Journey of a Mystic in Training

A Continuing Quest for Authentic Self Discovery and Expression

By
C. J. Cornelison

Illusrations by
Maria Pazos

Journey of a Mystic in Training
August 2010

Designed and produced by Hartley Publishing
Illustrations by Maria Pazos
Author photograph by Paul Glew

ISBN 978-0-615-39056-7

Hartley Publishing
Campbell, CA

Contents

Preface

This book is lovingly intended for folks who are open-minded and curious. It is by no means a pontification but rather a sharing of musings, ponderings and insights based on my life experiences to date. It is a snap shot in time, if you will, that encapsulates many of my currently held beliefs, perceptions, and philosophies regarding life; knowing full well that these will continue to evolve and expand as more life unfolds.

I believe that each of us has an innate hunger to wake up, to discern who we are and why we are here, and to partake in a continuing quest for authentic self discovery and expression. During this quest, this awakening process, we invariably find that there is much more to life than what meets the eye, or what we perceive with any of our five outward focused senses. As the process unfolds, we begin to routinely stretch our consciousness, and find ourselves delving beneath religious dogma to examine underlying spiritual principals and universal truths. We begin to experience synchronicity and a palpable sense of unity with increasing frequency. We begin to satiate our inherent thirst for enlightenment, and discover that enlightenment is not a static destination but rather a dynamic realm of limitless exploration. As the journey unfolds we soon realize that we are following in the footsteps of all the mystics that have gone before us. We are indeed mystics in training, and this quest for an enlightened way of being, fueled by inspiration, is the birthright of anyone who chooses to engage in it.

As a matter of definition, let me be clear from the beginning. A mystic is not someone who checks out from life, engages primarily in naval gazing and dwells exclusively in the transcendent experience. Rather, a true mystic develops a genuine mastery of life, recognizing that both the human and transcendent experiences are precious and that we have been given the capacity and a mandate to experience both fully.

Interestingly, the clarity of purpose and intent of this book didn't fully reveal itself to me until long after the chapters had been written and I was working with my publishing advisor and friend Lee Hartley. I use the wording "reveal itself to me" deliberately because this truly was an inspired endeavor. In fact, when I began this undertaking it was one of those situations where I was feeling called to do something, yet I didn't have a clue as to the how or the why of it. I had never written a book and it wasn't obvious how it was going to happen, but I knew that it was something that I was supposed to do. I could hear a song of uncertainty playing in my mind; yet rising above the chorus of doubt was a gentle, reassuring voice whispering, "You can do this! Just start writing, the ideas will come and the words will flow." It reminded me of the character Dory from the film Nemo, singing "just keep swimming, just keep swimming..." No doubt by this comment you've correctly ascertained that I do have young children, and, like many parents these days, I've had the distinct pleasure of watching many a fine Disney film more times than I would probably choose on my own accord. That being said, at least one thing was clear from the outset. I realized that writing this book was an opportunity to take a leap of faith, to trust that inner guiding voice ("just start writing, just start writing..."), and to follow that source of inspiration to wherever it may lead.

Although I'd never written a book before, I'd always enjoyed writing and often found it to be the most effective way for me to articulate my thoughts. Often when I have many incomplete or unclear thoughts swimming through my mind, writing helps me to make sense of these thoughts and then I'm able to release them and move on. So, what then to write about? I had written letters of encouragement to loved ones experiencing rough times. Similarly, I had shared thoughts, perspectives, spiritual and philosophical concepts with various friends and family members. Some of these dear ones had developed ways of being that seem to perpetuate a certain amount of chronic suffering in their lives. So I shared my ideas in the hope that these individuals may recognize that if they are not happy with their lives, they have the power to change their experience. Always, I strived to do this in a manner that was free of judgment and was presented merely as a loving gift for their consideration.

At first, none of these individual writings seemed like a basis for an entire book. Yet, when I considered all of them together, it occurred to me that I had the meager beginnings of a body of work that could serve as a good barometer of where I was on my spiritual journey, my mystical journey, my life journey. So starting from there, what unfolded, and what you shall soon read in the chapters ahead, is a collection of musings, ponderings and insights that are presented as food for thought to stimulate some of your own.

Let us begin then, and keep in mind that life is indeed a journey. We all know how it begins and how it ends. It's the in-between part that can be truly magical. It is the reason why we came into this physical incarnation in the first place. Each of us is here to experience life in ways that have never been experienced before. We are like grains of sand on an endless beach, each unique, yet each an integral part of a bigger whole.

Musings

*As I began the pursuit of re-discovering
myself, I found God in the process.
And, as I searched to find a God that
made sense to my head
and my heart, I found myself.*

The
Journey
Begins

*In life there are
no final destinations,
only points along an endless journey*

The Wake-up Call

Often it seems a spiritual awakening is precipitated by a cathartic experience of sorts. You hit a low point in your life and find that your routine ways of going about your business no longer seem effective. Try as you might, the downward spiral continues until you hit bottom, and with a sense of frustration and desperation you find yourself crying out "There's got to be a better way!" Such was the case for me in 1994 when I entered my 31st year of life. At that point, I had crafted what society would define as a successful life. I had a fascinating and promising career as research scientist/engineer working for NASA; I owned a charming home in a lovely, San Francisco bay area neighborhood; I had married a woman who was equally successful in her career, and we had a wonderful three year old son. It was the prototypical American dream. Yet, there was an unmistakable emptiness inside me that no amount of material success could satisfy. In addition, it seemed that by fully capitulating to societal, marital and familial expectations, I had completely lost myself in the process. It was the beginning of an existential identity crisis or what some might call a period of divine discontent.

Peeling Back the Layers

The root cause of this discontent was not readily apparent to me at the time. Like many folks who are spiritually asleep, my perceptions were based primarily on outward appearances and superficial details. For instance, from a surface level perspective it was clear that my wife and I had married at a young age, and we were steadily growing apart. As is often the case seemingly irresolvable frustrations had intensified as the years

3

passed. Without going into excessive details, one way to capture the context of our situation is as follows. In his book *How to be an Adult in Relationships*, David Richo lists five keys to a successful, loving relationship: attention, acceptance, appreciation, affection and allowing. When all of these are present everything naturally falls into place. However, when there are issues in one or more of these areas, problems usually arise. Suffice it to say my wife and I had significant issues in all of these areas.

To make matters even more interesting, my way of being at the time was one of head dominance and heart suppression. Often, my heartfelt responses were overridden or superseded by intellectual rationalizations. Likewise, my intuition was chiefly ignored or unnoticed. Not surprisingly I was in a relationship where my partner treated me in ways that were similar to how I treated myself. My intention here is not to point fingers of blame, for it always takes two to tango, but rather to further convey that my wife and I were two markedly different people, on two very different trajectories. Furthermore, it was the resulting emotional "hitting bottom" that served as the tipping point to jump-start my journey of awakening.

With the benefits of hindsight and an expanded perspective, I now realize that for every story such as this, there is a profusion of superficial details that define it. Yet, if we endeavor to peel back the layers and peer beneath the story and its details, we are certain to find that there are deeper processes stirring that serve to drive it. Thus the story is just an outward expression of deeper processes, that aren't necessarily obvious. Looking beyond my story, I now realize that my soul was yearning for attention and I was being called to forge an integrated way of being built upon a harmonious union of my head and heart. In other words, my authentic self was craving to be rediscovered and expressed.

As further evidence of this, during this time I would often lay awake at night contemplating the age-old, big questions: Who am I and why am I here? What is the purpose of life? Where did I come from and where will I go when I die? Who and what is God? I had no satisfying answers. In fact, I started to develop a suspicion that the main reason that society seemingly encourages a state of incessant busy-ness and perpetual doing, is simply to distract us from having to entertain questions such as these. These questions cannot be answered by way of materialism. So, like many individuals, this wake-up call, by way of catharsis, began to activate a desire within me to dive into the realm of the spiritual.

New Beginnings

Within a year I was divorced, shared joint custody of my son, was sleeping on a friend's futon, and had far fewer material possessions and financial assets. However, my journey of awakening had officially begun. Soon thereafter I found myself in a new relationship with a beautiful, inspiring woman who was equally spiritually curious, and whom I would eventually marry and together we would have three beautiful children. For the first time in my life I felt completely supported and encouraged to discover my authentic self and to follow my dreams.

Before proceeding to the next chapter, I would be remiss if I did not mention that my ex-wife happily remarried in 1996. She and her husband are a wonderful match and they have forged a beautiful life together. Also, our son is now attending

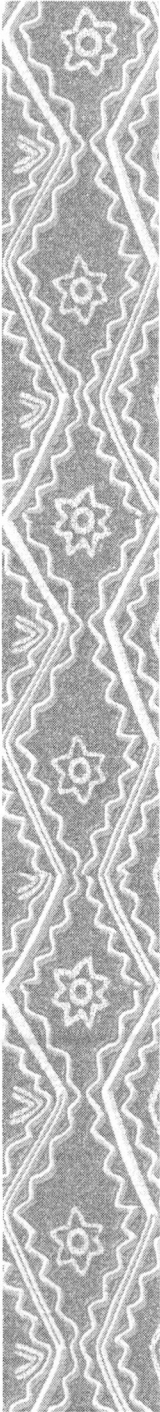

college and pursuing a pre-law degree. Now that the emotional upheavals have long since dissipated, I can honestly look back upon our relationship, divorce included, as a blessing that not only resulted in the birth of our son, but also catalyzed tremendous growth and personal development for both of us. One thing that I learned from the experience is that life has a way of continually providing opportunities through our situations, circumstances and relationships to stimulate our growth and evolution. Contrary to the popular axiom, "opportunity knocks only once," the reality is "opportunity is forever knocking yet it does so in continuously varying ways so that we may eventually heed its call."

Native
American
Traditions

*The world is a big place,
yet truth is truth no matter
where you are!*

The Good Red Road

Prior to my wake-up call, I had spent the majority of my life spiritually asleep or unconscious. In my youth I had walked the Catholic path for a number of years, and although it's a beautiful and popular faith that is steeped in history and tradition, it never really resonated with me. Likewise, during my early adult years I experienced other denominations of Christianity, and although I developed a tremendous veneration for Jesus and his teachings, none of these religions truly struck a cord with me. I decided that religion simply wasn't for me.

As 1994 drew to a close, I started experiencing a strong desire to reconnect with my father and to learn more about my Native American ancestry. My parents had separated when I was four years old and my father then moved to Canada to pursue a career opportunity. After a rather contentious divorce and a nasty custody battle, my mother was ultimately awarded full custody. The result being, I didn't have any contact or interaction with my father after that. As I began searching for his whereabouts, I also began immersing myself in Native American spiritual traditions. I poured over books by Black Elk, John Redtail Freesoul, Michael Garret and others who tried to document the ways and wisdom that had been passed down orally through the generations. I started putting their teachings into practice, and spent many a fine day wandering through forests or along secluded beaches to set up my medicine wheel and meditate for hours, becoming one with my environment, one with God. I had discovered the good red road, and at long last I had finally found a faith tradition that really resonated with me, and sung to both my head and my heart.

What is the "red road" you ask? It is a Native American term for a way of being, a way of doing, a way of life. One who walks the red road is one who is steeped in the recognition of the interconnectedness of all of creation, both animate and inanimate, and moves through life with a reverence and respect for all of existence. Such an individual is said to walk strongly yet softly upon the Earth. Such an individual consciously forges a life built upon principles of order, balance and harmony and with an intention of continuously discovering, developing and sharing his or her innate gifts and talents with the world. From the Native American perspective, there is no delineation between spiritual and ordinary matters. Everything in life is viewed as spiritual for all facets of life are infused with Spirit, the Great Spirit. Thus, the red road is a spiritual path, a mystical path, and walking the red road is the pursuit of finding one's place and purpose in the universe. The red road is open to all who are drawn to it regardless of cultural or religious background. Having said this, the chapters in this book stem from musings, ponderings and insights that have occurred to me while walking this path. You can think of them as rest stops along the good red road.

In 2001 I succeed at last in tracking down my father. Unfortunately it was a year after he had passed away. Needless to say I was deeply saddened, yet the emerging enlightened perspective I was acquiring by way of Native American traditions allowed me to embrace the grieving and healing processes. Soon I felt a deeper connection with my father than I had since I was a four-year-old little boy living in Thousand Oaks California. As my journey of awakening continued, Native American traditions proved to be a wellspring for the unfoldment of my consciousness. During this time in my life I learned and experienced much.

Familiar lessons from a not so Familiar Tradition

There are over 500 Nations or Native American tribes in North America with over 150 different languages. As such, there are subtle differences in the details of the spiritual traditions between these tribes, similar to the differences in various denominations of Christianity. However, the following universal beliefs are common to all tribes.

There is one Great Spirit in and throughout every thing. The Great Spirit exists in all people, all plants, all creatures on land, in water or air, the ground on which we walk, the air that we breathe, and the water we drink. It's in the sun, the moon and the heavens above. There is no place in this vast universe in which the Great Spirit does not dwell. In other words, the Great Spirit (God) is omnipresent.

We should not take more than we need. The Great Spirit dwells in everything and everything has a purpose. Thus, everything should be treated with respect. Contrary to the notion of dominion that is popular in some faith traditions, the Native American perspective does not subscribe to the belief that the earth and all its resources were created solely for humans to use to satisfy their wants and desires. Rather, as the species that has the greatest ability to affect the environment and other life on our planet, it is our duty and responsibility to be good stewards and to help foster harmony and balance so that all life can thrive. With great power comes great responsibility. This belief recognizes that we are all connected and there is no separation.

We should always give thanks for what we have and what we receive. To the Native American, gratitude is a way of life. It is a good vehicle to move us from "doing" to "being." Often we get so caught up with the doings of life we forget we are human beings, not human doings. We measure and judge folks by their social circumstances or occupations or material wealth, and we forget that everyone has a purpose and value simply by being alive.

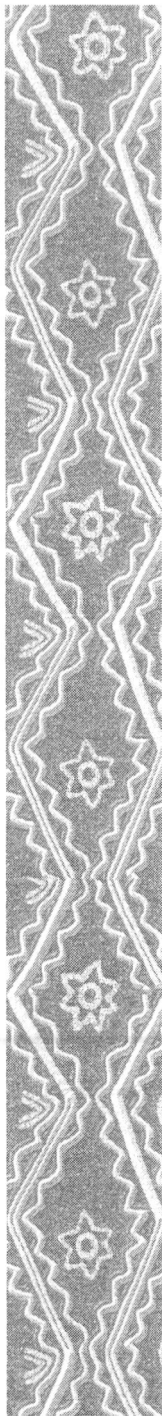

We should use all that we have. Once again the idea of waste is frowned upon since everything has purpose and is divine; the Great Spirit is at its core. Implied here also are the golden rule and compassion. In other words, be mindful of how you impact the world and affect the experiences of others.

We should give away all that we don't need. The principles of circulation and reciprocity are very important in the Native American way. At the surface is the recognition that during our life experience we tend to accumulate many things and over time we no longer have a need for many of these things. Thus, these things should be given away so others who have need for them can use them. Our ability to receive is forever tied to our ability to give. How can we receive any more if our hands are already full? Native American traditions believe that being grateful is the nature of all humans. The feeling that one experiences when one gives without the expectation of receiving something in return, other than the honor and joy of being able to give, is in harmony with our true nature. As Michael Garret puts it in his book *Walking on the Wind*, "It is a way of reaffirming one's connection with the natural flow of the Greater Circle of Life through an expression of wisdom, kindness and humility." What we consider to be our possessions in this life experience are really never owned by us. Eventually all possessions must be passed along to either someone else or back to Mother Earth.

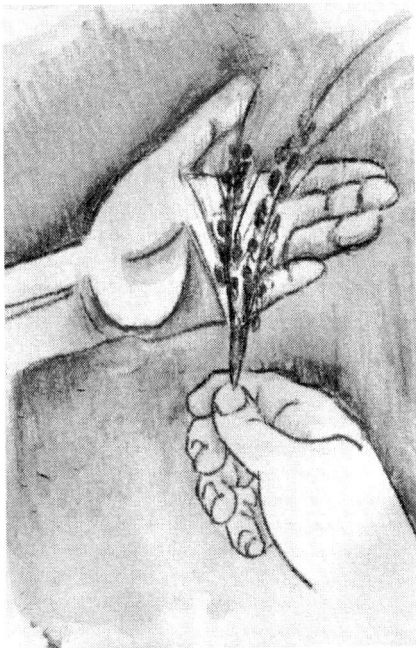

Everyone should be treated with respect, and dignity. We are spiritual beings having human experiences, and our human traits are to be accepted, respected and not judged. This quote by John Redtail Freesoul eloquently captures this idea: "Identity transcends race and ethnicity. While color and race are gifts given at birth and are to be accepted and respected, the soul cannot be confined within human made boundaries. The soul's nationality is spirit; its country is the universe."

As my awareness grows and I delve deeper into Native American traditions, I find that many of the concepts that resonate strongly with me are essentially the same as what I've been learning via other spiritual faith traditions. In some ways this should come as no surprise, after all, the world is a big place and the truth is the truth no matter where you are.

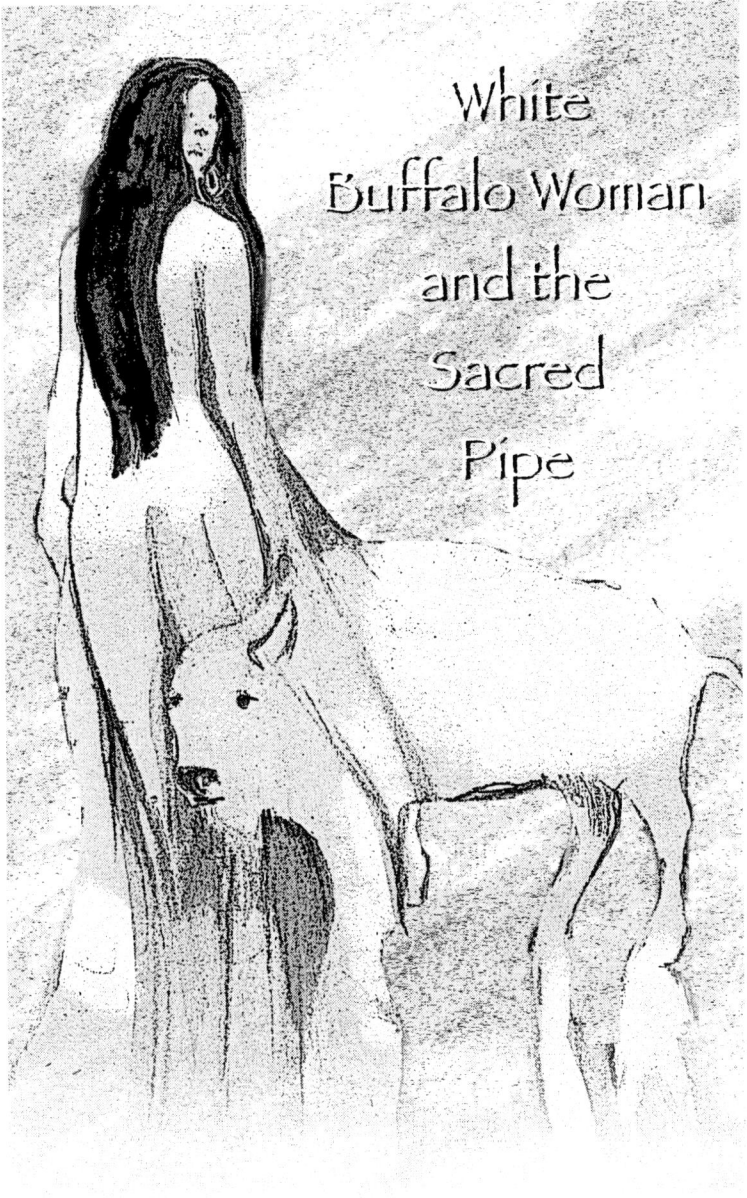

White Buffalo Woman and the Sacred Pipe

All paths can lead to God!

The native North American story of the White Buffalo Woman and the Sacred Pipe tends to be a bit of a mystery to those not well acquainted with Native American traditions and history. Yet, it is a story that stands side-by-side with those of Moses and the burning bush, Jesus rising on the third day, Buddha attaining enlightenment under the bodi tree, and Arjuna's conversation with Krishna. It is a story of divine revelation and inspiration that forever changed a nation, the native people of North America.

I have crossed paths with this story at different times in my life and have noticed that the amount and nature of the details vary depending upon who is telling it, yet the spirit of the story and truths underpinning it remain the same. There is an important lesson here; truth most often resides beneath the surface. Whether a story is passed on through the millennia orally, or via written text that is translated and reinterpreted as word meanings change, the literal details to a story can vary dramatically. The story then becomes a mere vehicle for the underlying truth. Therefore, one must be willing to look beyond surface literal translations to glean the pearls of wisdom contained within. Our receptivity and ability to explore and recognize these depths evolves as our consciousness evolves. Here is my recollection of the story of the White Buffalo Woman and the Sacred Pipe and some of the embedded truths I have discovered in it.

White Buffalo Woman and the Sacred Pipe

The story begins ages ago, perhaps during the time of Jesus or Buddha or earlier still. Two young men had been hunting for several days without success. As they walked towards a low-lying hill, in the distance they noticed a figure approaching. As the figure drew nearer they recognized it to be a beautiful young woman dressed in white buckskin. The young men were enchanted by her beauty, and the feeling of power and purpose that emanated from her.

One young man became filled with lustful desire, the other with awe and wonder. The first young man, intent on satisfying his desire, sprinted up the path toward the approaching woman. However, upon reaching her he was immediately struck down. The second young man, having been true to his nature, stood silently as the woman approached. With a smile on her face, she kindly asked him to go to his people and inform them that she would return in several days with a holy gift and guidance. The woman then turned and walked away in the direction from which she came. In the distance, she stopped, turned into a white buffalo calf and then disappeared. Per her instruction, the young man returned to his people, informed them of the coming of this holy woman, and they prepared for her arrival.

As promised, the mysterious White Buffalo Woman arrived four days later carrying a bundle, which proved to be the first sacred pipe (chanunpa). She spent several days with the people teaching them many things. Beginning first with

The lesson of the first young man:

Different accounts of the story describe the fall of the first young man in a variety of ways. Some say he was struck by lightning, others say a cloud momentarily enveloped him and all that remained were his bones in a small pile on the ground, and still others say snakes consumed him. The specifics are unimportant. The lesson is that ignoring our true nature and allowing ourselves to become consumed or obsessed by our desires can be our undoing. Or, as recognized in Buddhist traditions, attachment to our desires can cause us much suffering.

the pipe, she explained that it is both symbolic as well as a tool of great power. She explained that all things are connected, the Great Spirit (Wakan Tanka) resides everywhere in all things at all times, and one way to see this is by recognizing that all things on Mother Earth breathe, including animals, plants, rocks, oceans and people. The air circulates in and throughout everything. The air can be thought of as the breath of the Great Spirit. By taking the sacred tobacco smoke into our mouths (not lungs) and exhaling it, it makes the breath of the Invisible One visible. This is good medicine and a powerful reminder of the divine essence that exists in all things. The pipe and its proper use remind us of this truth.

She then taught the people to recognize the unique importance of all members of the tribe; men, women and children. This restored balance and equality to a society that had become rather male-dominated. She taught them songs, prayers, new ways to prepare and cook food, and the art of pipe making. Lastly, she taught them seven sacred rites or ceremonies.

The first was the sweat lodge, or purification ceremony. The second was the naming ceremony, for naming

The experience of the second young man:

It is implied that the second young man could sense from the beginning that there was something very special and obviously holy about the Woman in White. Some accounts suggest that when she looked into his eyes and spoke to him, he then recognized her as the Great Spirit in human form. This young man's experience is very much like that of Arjuna when he first recognized the identity of Krishna in the Bhagavad-Gita.

children. The third was the healing ceremony and how to use various herbs and plants to cure illnesses. The fourth was the adoption or making of relatives ceremony. The fifth was the marriage ceremony. The sixth was the vision quest. And the seventh was the sundance ceremony, which symbolizes the continuity between life and death (recognizing that nothing really ever dies).

After four days, near sunset, the White Buffalo Woman bid goodbye to the people and said, "I shall see you again." She walked away in the same direction from which she came. As she neared the top of a nearby rise, with the setting sun behind her she stopped and turned into a white buffalo calf before disappearing from view.

On some of the ceremonies: Some accounts of the story say the Woman in White taught the ceremonies to the people, others say she explained that they would be taught seven sacred rites via divine inspiration and through proper use of the pipe. Once again the specifics are unimportant. What it important is that it was recognized long ago that rituals are very useful tools for developing spiritual awareness. The intention of the purification (sweat) ceremony is to not only rid the body of toxins, but to rid the mind of thoughts that no longer serve you. It is but one way to focus on our connection to Spirit, by putting God first. Similarly, the vision quest involves going alone to a sacred place with a blanket, pipe and water for one to four days to engage in intense meditating, praying and fasting to maximize receptivity to and communion with the divine. It is yet another way. The sundance ceremony is used to represent the unending cycle of birth and death. It involves praying, fasting, purifying, dancing, meditating and in the traditional form there are elements of piercing and flesh offering. Ritualistic self torture is too extreme for my taste. It reminds me of Opus Dei and Christianity. Newer versions of the sundance ceremony that forego the piercing and flesh offering steps suit me fine.

The pipe as symbol and tool: As symbol, the pipe (stone bowl, wooden stem, and all of its decorations) represents the many aspects and expressions of the Great Spirit. As such, it is symbolic of the masculine and feminine, those things that change very slowly (as represented by the stone of the bowl) and those that change rapidly (as represented the wood of the stem). Everything we see in the universe is the Great Spirit in physical form and yet the Great Spirit comprises the invisible realm as well. As a tool we can use the pipe to visualize something that is usually invisible, breath. This reminds us of our connection to all things seen and unseen and provides a useful tool in developing an even deeper relationship to the Great Spirit through prayer and meditation.

To this day, the pipe and the white buffalo are two of the most revered symbols in Native American spiritual traditions, analogous to the crucifix in Christianity and the Star of David in Judaism. Also, what is believed to be the original sacred pipe brought to the people by the White Buffalo Woman (known as the White Buffalo Calf Pipe) is kept in a sacred place on the Cheyenne River Indian Reservation in South Dakota.

The
Medicine
Wheel

Rituals and ceremonies
can be useful tools for worship,
but they themselves should never
be worshiped

The medicine wheel has been a mainstay in Native American spiritual traditions for several millennia. Many believe that it predates the coming of the White Buffalo Woman and the use of the pipe. Like the pipe, it is both symbolic and a tool, and it provides the user a means to better understand life, themselves and their relationship to and awareness of the Great Spirit (God). For me, the medicine wheel was the cornerstone of my spiritual practice for the better part of a decade. Since that time I have joined a new-thought ancient-wisdom spiritual community and have expanded my spiritual practice to include a variety of forms of meditation, spiritual study, affirmative prayer and selfless service. Although I don't use the medicine wheel as frequently these days, it remains a steadfast part of my life. It is like a beloved friend that I can always rely on to help me re-attune my perceptions and refocus my perspectives. It is my honor to share with you what I have learned about the medicine wheel and how to set one up and use it. In my experience, I realize that I have only scratched the surface in discovering all that it has to offer, but this has made a significant impact in my life. Perhaps it will in yours.

The Medicine Wheel as Symbol

At its core the medicine wheel is a circle, a circle superimposed upon a cross (not a crucifix), thus marking its center and four equidistant or cardinal directions. Each of these cardinal directions corresponds to the points on a compass or the east, south, west and north winds. The center represents the unchanging, the timeless, the eternal from which all things emanate and return. Conversely, the circle represents that which is forever changing, the nature of existence in the physical realm and, in particular, occurrences that are cyclical in nature. The cardinal directions can be related to points along these cyclical paths. Such occurrences include the seasons (spring, summer, fall and winter), the time of day (sunrise, noon, sunset, and midnight), the phases of the moon (1st quarter, full, 3rd quarter and new), the time of life (infancy, youth, adulthood and elderhood) during our human incarnation, and the phases of existence (in the womb, after the womb, beyond the body and before the womb) as our souls journey through limitless incarnations.

In addition, certain colors (yellow, red, black and white), elements (fire, earth, air and water), plants, animals, minerals and perspectives (enlightenment, subjectivity, introspection and objectivity) are associated with each of the cardinal directions. Still another aspect of life that the circular form of the medicine wheel reminds us of is that of duality. Seemingly opposites (hot vs. cold, dark vs. light, right vs. wrong, condemnation vs. forgiveness) appear to be distinct entities that are separate in some linear fashion, when in fact they are simply opposite sides of a common circle. One gives rise or leads to the other, and there is no beginning or end. One cannot be perceived without the other. The medicine wheel as symbol reminds us of this circular connection, and the cyclical nature that is so prevalent in the universe.

The Medicine Wheel as Tool

When you set up a medicine wheel with proper intention, you effectively create a sacred space with an atmosphere of receptivity. Traditionally, folks meditate in this space or they can pray

or contemplate various life issues and situations. For example, meditating within the wheel provides an opportunity to glean divine insight as to the nature of the Great Spirit, various aspects of the universe and especially oneself. The medicine wheel provides a vehicle to further develop one's relationship to and awareness of God and all things in this vast universe. It is a means to expand one's consciousness. When faced with certain decisions, problems or life issues, contemplating these situations using the perspectives of the four directions can yield valuable guidance in determining next steps, instill a better understanding, and identify underlying causes and ramifications. It is said that the answer to any question and the solution to any problem lies within each of us. Accessing this knowing, this truth, is done by tapping into your divine essence. Within this space of receptivity, you begin to realize and recognize that you are the Great Spirit in form, and yet God is still much more. You are connected to, and an individualized expression of, the infinite all knowing Creator. By using the medicine wheel, you can uncover, discover, recover and remember this connection.

Setting up a Medicine Wheel

Setting up a medicine wheel is a ceremony, a ritual, the intent of which is to cultivate an ever-deepening relationship with God and to expand one's consciousness. The goal of any such ceremony is to focus your attention on the intention, by temporarily suspending the distractions of everyday life occurrences. As is the case with all rituals the details of the steps that are followed are not particularly important.

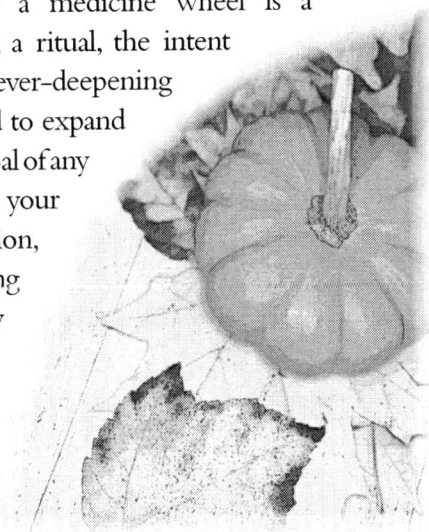

It's all about intention. However, performing the steps consistently is important, because cultivating a relationship with God or expanding one's consciousness is most successfully accomplished if it's done with consistency. It's analogous to becoming a good musician or athlete. Consistent practice produces the best results. Any accomplished musician or athlete practices their skill frequently and consistently. So, whenever you are engaging in a ritual such as this, follow whatever steps work best for you, but do so consistently. This will produce the best and most satisfying results.

To set up your medicine wheel, gather five stones which will be used to mark each of the four cardinal directions plus the center. Each stone should be a representative color. The colors that I learned are typical of some of the Plains tribes such as the Lakota, Cheyenne, and Arapahoe. The color for the center stone is blue, the color we see when we look to sky above. The vast blue sky reminds us of the infinite nature of the Creator. The color for the east is yellow or gold, which reminds us of the warm rays of the sunrise and the illumination that comes with enlightenment. The color for the south is red or green, which reminds us of the heat of the mid-day summer sun, and the mature plants that sprang to life in the spring and are now thriving. The color for the west is black, which reminds us of the darkness that follows the sunset, and the comforting darkness of solitude and introspection. The color for the north is white, which reminds us of the snows of winter, as well as purity and objectivity. Quite often you can find stones of these colors in nature. If you make finding such stones your intention, and keep alert during your walks in nature, such stones will find you. That is, you will be drawn to them and

notice them. Give it a try. If this doesn't work to your satisfaction you can always paint or decorate five ordinary stones with the appropriate colors.

Next you will need to gather some dry red cedar or sage leaves plus a small bowl or shell that they can be burned in for smudging. Once you have gathered your stones and smudging supplies, you are ready to begin. Although you can set up a medicine wheel anywhere, most people enjoy a secluded, pristine location in nature where you feel a strong connection to your surroundings. This can be on a beach, in a forest, on a mountain top, in a meadow, or along a riverbank. Journey to such a location, and when you arrive burn some of the sage or cedar leaves in your smudging pot. Bathe the stones and your body in the purifying smoke. Enjoy the sweet scent. In a way, smudging is a mini ceremony in and of itself. While it is often viewed as a simple purification step (the smoke is believed to dispel negative energies, thoughts, spirits, etc.) it is also a powerful metaphor. As the sage or cedar leaves burn, they are transformed into smoke which then dissipates. During this process the visible becomes the invisible. Similarly, in our use of the medicine wheel we can transcend the human experience to the divine. Our focus on human matters shifts to divine recognition and communion. This metaphor allows us to recognize that cycles and patterns quite often echo one another.

At the spot where you wish to set up your medicine wheel, begin by entering the wheel from the east and walk to the center. Hold your blue stone aloft and give thanks to the Great Spirit for the gift of life. Place it on the ground to mark the center of your wheel and then take seven steps to the east. Hold your yellow stone aloft and give thanks for the sunrise, the beginning of a new day, springtime and all the gifts of

the east. Place the yellow stone on the ground and return to the center. Next take seven steps to the south and hold your red stone aloft. Give thanks for the strong noon sun, the warmth of summer, and all of the gifts of the south. Place the red stone on the ground and return once again to the center. Then take seven steps to the west and hold your black stone aloft. Give thanks for the sunset, the end of a beautiful day and the beginning of a wonderful evening, autumn and all the gifts of the west. Place the black stone on the ground and return once again to the center. Finally, take seven steps to the north and hold your white stone aloft. Give thanks for midnight, the majesty of the night sky, winter and all the gifts of the north. Place the white stone on the ground and return once again to the center. Give thanks to the wisdom of the fours directions (winds) and all that exists in this amazing universe.

Sit down in the center and take seven deep cleansing breaths. Meditate, focusing on your breath, for about ten minutes. Steadily calm your mind and whenever thoughts distract you, gently return your attention to your breath. After ten minutes or so, see which direction you feel called to visit. Get up and move from the center to that point on the wheel. If you don't feel drawn to any particular direction then stay in the center until you do (if you do). Continue to meditate, gradually settling your thoughts, so that you can experience the silence between them and connect with the Great Spirit. Alternatively, you can move about the wheel to contemplate a problem or life situation using the various perspectives each direction has to offer. In any case, you are making yourself receptive to divine

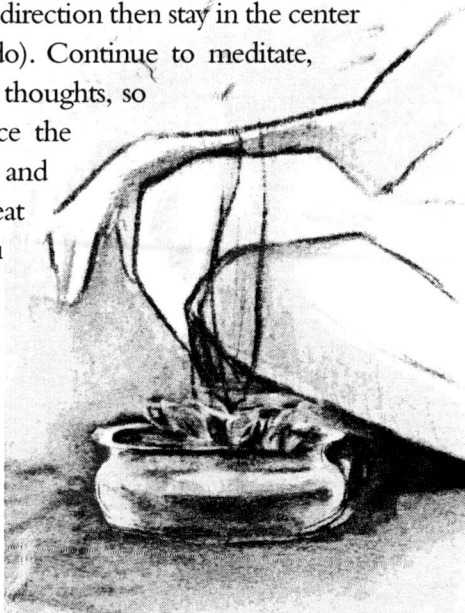

inspiration and guidance. Where you go from here is up to you. Have fun with it!

When moving about the wheel to different locations, always remember to pass through the center. The purpose of this traditional step is to remind us that ultimately everything comes from and returns to the Creator. Leaving and re-entering the medicine wheel is always done through the East.

When you have finished your meditation, contemplation or prayers, and you wish to take down your medicine wheel, the steps are similar to those you followed during the set up. Begin at the center and proceed to the east. Pick up the yellow stone and once again give thanks, then return to the center. Proceed to the south and so on in a "sun-wise" procession. Lastly pick up the blue center stone, give thanks to the Great Spirit and exit to the east. The ceremony is now complete.

This is the medicine wheel ceremony as I have learned it. Some tribes associate different colors, animals, perspectives, and so on with each of the cardinal directions. This reminds us not to get lost in the details. It's the intention behind the ceremony that is truly important, and practicing it with consistency is what makes it effective. The medicine wheel has been in use since antiquity and it remains a powerful and effective symbol and tool. It is one way, of which there are many, to expand your consciousness and cultivate an ever deepening relationship with God. Good luck, and may you enjoy your experiences with it.

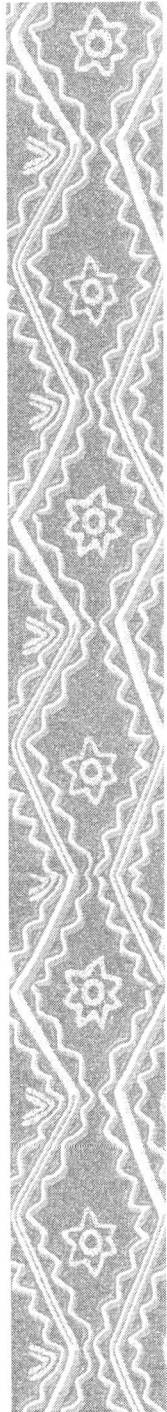

Mystical Experiences

God has never stopped talking, but many folks have forgotten how to listen

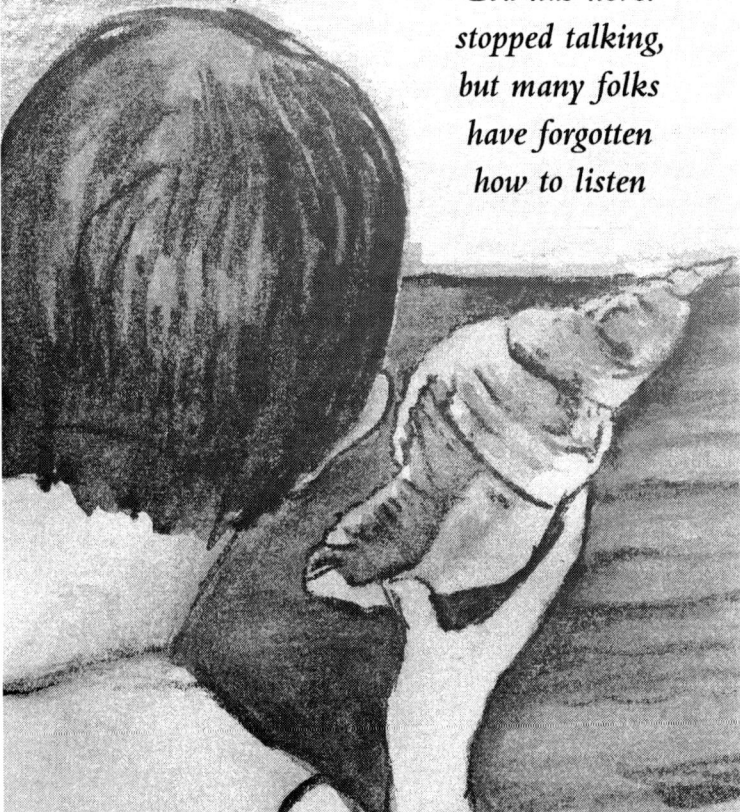

When I was a child, a popular verbal exchange would begin with the question, "What is jazz?" To this the response was something like, "I don't know how to define it, but I know it when I hear it." Defining what a mystical experience is can be similarly elusive but you know it when it happens to you. The difficulty in developing a simple definition for a "mystical experience" is probably that such an experience tends to be imbued with emotion, feeling and a level of knowing that can be difficult to express with words. I have had a variety of what I believe to be mystical experiences. Some were profound, some were subtle, each was unique, and yet each shared some common characteristics. Based on these personal experiences, I would offer the following definition.

First and foremost, a mystical experience is an experience of the divine. Specifically, it involves awareness and recognition of the divine in form around you, and a sense of connection to it. Often, there is a sudden feeling that you are a part of something much bigger than your mind, body, your "human" being. You are one with your surroundings, with everything, with God. There can often be revelation, epiphany, a "eureka" moment where there is a new level of understanding, a knowing of truth that suddenly crystallizes. There can be a sense of transcendence from believing to knowing. Any or all of these things can occur, and it leaves you with a feeling of euphoria, with the hair standing up on the back of your neck. At least this has been my experience, and having said that, I've had three mystical experiences I would like to share with you.

The Lessons of Hawk Medicine

It was a blustery, sunny, autumn day with very few clouds in the sky. The wind was blowing from the north and although it would slow at times and gust at others, it was more or less constant. I made my way to a secluded beach that had become like a second home to me. This area was most easily accessible when the tide was low, and I could typically expect to spend several hours there without seeing another person. I stopped at a tranquil spot and set up my medicine wheel in the usual fashion, marking the center and the four cardinal directions (east, south, west and then north). To the west lay the ocean, to the east the tall sandstone cliffs and to the north and south lay long stretches of pristine shoreline washed clean from the recently retreating tide.

On this particular day I was feeling tired and scattered and in need of some centering, so I decided to begin meditating at the center of my medicine wheel and go from there. Right away I noticed that my mind was bustling with activity and I was finding it difficult to still my thoughts. Soon I was also having difficulty staying awake. Just when my mind would begin to quiet down I'd start to nod off. After about 45 minutes or so I thought, "Man! This isn't going so well. Either my head is filled with chatter or I'm drifting off to sleep. Maybe I should pack up and go home?" Then, a thought suddenly occurred to me, "Why fight it? Just take a nap." It was like a small voice whispering in my ear, and I thought, "Why not? That's a great idea!" So I laid down in the soft sand in the center of the wheel, facing the sky with my head to the north, feet to the south and arms spread wide. I could feel the warmth of the sun upon my skin and hear the soothing sound of the waves and the swirling wind. In almost no time I drifted off to the most comfortable sleep I'd had in days.

I awoke some time later with an overwhelming sensation that somebody was watching me. I opened my eyes, and there, hovering not more than 15 feet above me, like a mirror image (head to the north, tail to the south

and wings spread wide), was a big beautiful red-tail hawk. We stared at each other for what seemed like minutes and then she departed. I've always been an animal lover and in particular I've always had a fondness for red-tail hawks. They are my favorite species of bird and I've always felt a strong connection to them, even before I began exploring Native American traditions. What particularly struck me about this hawk was an undeniable feeling of warmth and familiarity, like the feeling you get when you cross paths with a loved one you haven't seen in some time. Until then, I had never felt a connection quite like this with a non-human before.

I watched as she deftly ascended toward the top of the cliff face, riding a thermal updraft, and then glided back down only to rise up again. As she did this time and again she moved steadily northward, into the direction from whence the wind was blowing, with grace and minimal effort. Soon she faded from view and I shifted my attention toward the water and became aware of many pelicans, seagulls and other shorebirds that were all flying northward as well. In contrast, however, these other birds were struggling with great effort to make headway in their northerly procession. All of these winged ones had the same destination in mind yet for one the journey was relatively easy, and for the others it was quite difficult. It was at this time that the "eureka" moment struck me. I was clearly observing a metaphor for life. "Life can be easy or difficult depending upon the choices we make!" We can emulate the hawk or the other birds. In either case we will get to where we are going, only one path will get us there easily, and the other will be a struggle. How many times do we find ourselves complaining about life's difficulties or busyness and fail to realize it's largely a product of our choices? This is an important lesson in Hawk medicine.

Another bit of insight that I learned from my hawk friend that day was the importance of "surrender" and the sense of freedom and liberation that comes with it. So often in our attempt to get to a final destination or to obtain a certain result, we narrowly focus our efforts on what we perceive to be the one and only way. We myopically struggle and fight to stay the course and consequently find the journey to be quite difficult. If we simply let go of trying to control the situation and learn to work in concert with all the elements (as opposed to struggling against them), more often than not, we will get to where we wish with much less grief and having experienced a much more enjoyable journey. Surrender is a multifaceted, paradoxical life skill that is so beneficial if used or mastered. On the surface it seems like you are giving up control and yet in the end you find yourself in complete control. Typically, what you find is that by surrendering you let go of those things you really don't have control of, and you refocus your energy on those things you do have control over. Furthermore, you do so in a cooperative manner and thereby gravitate toward win-win situations.

A Visitor from the West

Summer days along the California mid-coast are typically cool and foggy, but this day was one of those cherished exceptions that coastal dwellers live for: warm temperatures with clear blue skies and gentle breezes. It was an incredible day to be alive. I had returned to my secluded beach once again to set up my medicine wheel and meditate, feel my connection to nature, commune with the Great Spirit, and possibly find guidance and answers to various life situations and questions. I set up my medicine wheel in the usual fashion and on this day I was feeling drawn to spend time in the west, a direction that is affiliated with introspection.

As I settled into the western part of my wheel, my attention was drawn to a reef located about 50 yards offshore that was recently exposed by the receding tide. It was occupied by dozens of sea lions that were taking a break from their daily foraging activities to sun themselves and rest. I observed this peaceful scene for several moments and then closed my eyes, took several deep breaths, and began meditating. After awhile, I slipped into a dream. In this dream I was sitting in the same spot meditating when I felt the need to open my eyes. Upon doing so, I was startled to see a very large and menacing Native American fellow standing directly in front of me staring down at me. He was roughly 6' 5" tall and was wearing a long black robe of some animal fur. He sat down just in front of me, staring intensely into my eyes, still towering above me even though he was sitting. Needless to say I was feeling rather uncomfortable with this imposing, if not scary, figure just a few feet away. The words that swirled through my mind were "Yikes! I think I'm about to get my ass kicked." Then all of a sudden he broke into a huge smile and the whole vibe of the moment changed from foreboding to warmth and love. This person, whom I now believe to be a spirit keeper (Native American equivalent of an angel) said "Chuck, the lesson that I am sharing with you today is that not everything is as it appears. So don't be too quick to judge or jump to conclusions. You may have heard this wisdom expressed in other ways such as: looks can be deceiving, or don't judge a book by its cover. In any case, the truth is the same and it is good medicine. Remember this and it will serve you well." It seemed to take me awhile to get my mouth to work but finally I managed to say "Thank you for sharing that." He continued to smile and said, "Let's close our eyes and meditate on this."

In the dream I closed my eyes and began to ponder what he had said and what had just happened. Then I awoke and opened my eyes only to find the spirit keeper was gone. I looked around and thought, "Wow! That was quite a dream. The Great Spirit certainly has interesting ways in which to communicate." Then I noticed the sand in front of me and my jaw dropped. It was disturbed as if someone had been sitting just outside my medicine wheel to the west! Had this really been a dream? I had arrived at this stretch of beach just as the tide had gone out, and mine were the only tracks. I didn't recall venturing beyond the perimeter of my medicine wheel other than when I had entered from the east. So where did this disturbance come from? Then the truth of the day crystallized in my mind. "Not everything is as it appears. Don't be too quick to jump to conclusions." My mind began to swim with realization. I would do well to refrain from judging or at least delay making judgments, for often, my judgments are based on incomplete understanding. In addition, I should keep an open mind. Sometimes I get so attached to how something "should be" that I become oblivious to how it "could be." This leaves me blind to alternatives, many of which might be better than my expectation.

On this day I also became aware of an interesting facet of human behavior. The human mind is very adept at taking a handful of facts or observations and filling in the blanks with assumptions to create a complete storyline that seems to make sense. In a very short period of time it is no longer obvious what were the facts, and what were the assumptions. This can lead to some interesting situations including upset and conflict. For example, folks can form strong opinions or take offense based on what they perceive to be a true storyline. In fact, once they've bought into the storyline, a filter gets activated such that they become particularly sensitive to anything that confirms or supports the storyline. However, when more information becomes available it is quite often found that many of the assumptions were incorrect and, hence, the storyline was in error. Sadly, folks can spend a great deal of time and energy being upset or concerned about things that aren't or weren't true. Also, when folks receive additional information that doesn't support their original storyline, one of two things usually occurs: some open minded folks revise their storyline to incorporate the new information; and others try their best to dismiss or discredit the new information.

Having worked at NASA for over two decades, I've had numerous occasions wherein I've witnessed some extremely intelligent, well-meaning individuals conjure up some very elegant theories based on limited data. Yet, when more data becomes available these individuals can be very resistant to revising their theories. Their personal attachment often blinds them to the truth of the situation. However, the truth almost always prevails, and unfortunately it usually comes at a significant price. Interestingly, my frustration in dealing with these types of individuals was the main reason I was feeling compelled to sit in the west that fateful day. In so doing I developed a clearer understanding of why some folks do what they do and the perils of attachment. I'm reminded of an old saying, "The mind is a wonderful servant, but a terrible master!" In other words, receptivity to a paradigm shift leads to growth and freedom, whereas, resistance to a paradigm shift leads to stagnation and bondage.

Perhaps these truths came to me via the visitor from the west in a dream, perhaps not. Perhaps the disturbance in the sand was a physical trace of a spirit keeper that shared good medicine with me on that fine day or perhaps not. What is truly important is the truth of the message. Not everything is as it appears! So be patient and don't jump to conclusions.

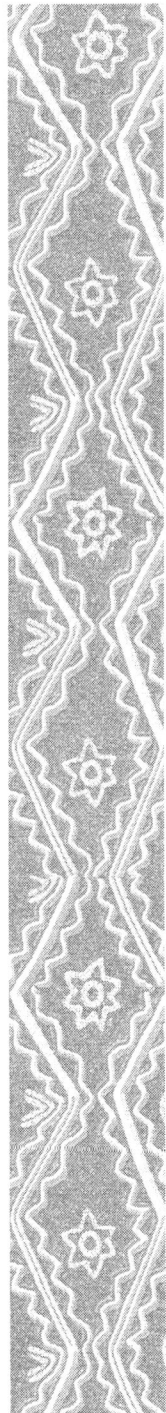

A Flat Tire Story

The third and final mystical experience I wish to share actually didn't involve the medicine wheel or the beach. I was leaving the San Jose Center for Spiritual Living after attending a "singing bowl" concert one evening. At the time I was not very well versed in chakras and such, or how various bowls resonate with these chakras and energy states, but I was feeling extremely relaxed and rejuvenated as I began my journey homeward. Seeing that my car was in need of fuel I planned to stop at a gas station. As I approached the stoplight just before the gas station, my car began to vibrate and pull to one side as is typical when you have a front tire going flat. I pulled up to the stoplight and thought, "Looks like I have a tire to change after I get some gas." When the light turned green, I limped through the intersection, into the station and up to a pump. I got out of my car and sure enough the left front tire looked flat and felt spongy to the touch.

Soon after I started filling my gas tank, a homeless man donning an old San Francisco Giants cap and a goatee strolled up to me and asked if I could spare any change. Still feeling the positive effects of the singing bowls I said sure, without hesitation, and pulled the remaining $5 bill out of my wallet and gave it to him. He immediately said, "Thank you so much, God bless you!" I said, "I am blessed, thank you and bless you, I hope it helps." He smiled, shook my hand and walked away. When the pump clicked off, I replaced my gas cap, returned the nozzle to the pump, grabbed my receipt and proceeded to drive over to the air and water station where I planned to change my tire. I got out of my car and I looked at my tire and it didn't look as flat as it had over by the pump. I thought maybe I can just add some air and it will get me home. So I grabbed my pressure gauge and much to my surprise it read 32 psi. My tire wasn't flat at all. The hair on the back of my neck stood up. What had just happened? The sound and feel when driving and the initial observation had me convinced that my tire was flat. However, it wasn't flat anymore. How did that happen? Also, where did that homeless guy go? He seemed to have disappeared back into the night.

To this day I still have no explanation, but my definition for "angel" is forever changed. I no longer think of angels as ethereal beings that descend from the heavens. I suppose they could be, but to me an angel is anyone or anything that unexpectedly does "good" in our lives without any expectation for compensation. They give graciously because it is their loving nature to do so. In this sense we all have the capacity to be angels to others. Any time we engage in a random act of kindness we are, in effect, an angel. I now realize that many angels have touched and continue to touch my life including my hawk friend, the spirit keeper from the west and the homeless man with the Giants cap and goatee. Similarly, when my wife first told me "I love you," and those occasions where I've woken up to find one of my children smiling at me and saying "Good morning daddy!" these are angels, too. Yes, it would appear that angels surround us and we get to play the role as well. Isn't life cool?

Ponderings

What's Your Take on God?

*Contrary to popular belief,
it takes a tremendous
amount of faith to
be an Atheist*

Mention the "G word" (God), not to be confused with the "G spot," in a crowd of folks and you are likely to get a mixture of reactions. Of course, mentioning the "G spot" is likely to garner a mixture of reactions as well, for it too is somewhat shrouded in mystery, but we'll save that topic for another time. Folks who are at a point in their lives wherein they have found a faith tradition that brings them a sense of joy and inner peace, tend to be very comfortable when somebody mentions God (or Spirit, the Universe, Goddess, Allah, The Great Spirit, Creator, Source, call it what you like). Other folks who have not had particularly joyous or fulfilling experiences with religion, or have yet to find a spiritual faith tradition that resonates with them (floats their boat, butters their bread, or...), tend to feel uncomfortable when someone drops a G-bomb, that is, mentions God. In addition, there are folks that consider themselves to be atheists and often either say or think things like "these God-squad types only use the idea of a God as a crutch to avoid dealing with reality."

During the course of my life I've reacted in "all of the above" ways at one time or another when the subject of God has been brought up. I've realized that my reaction at any particular moment had a lot to do with my understanding or definition of what God is and how God operates. Many cultures refer to God as the Great Mystery, and for good reason. Wrapping your mind around something that is omnipresent, omnipotent, omniscient, eternal, infinite, created a vast universe and is greater still, is no easy task and a pretty abstract concept. Yet, at some point in our lives most of us eventually ponder questions such as: Does God really exist? Where is God? What is God's nature? How does God work? We are offered a variety of answers from a variety of places, and eventually we develop a belief system that paints a picture, albeit incomplete and often fuzzy in our mind.

One popular God model is that of a bearded, male figure ruling from distant heavens that is quick to judge and punish. Another is that of a purely loving presence that is everywhere, in all things, at all times, and created a Universe of cause and effect where there is no judgment on Its part. Still others view God as not a person or consciousness, but rather the fundamental mechanisms and processes that drive the universe. It is not unusual that our life experiences cause us to continually revise and redefine our beliefs about God. For example, when I hear folks say they are questioning their faith in God, I think it's more accurate to say they are questioning their beliefs about God. If God is infinite, it makes perfect sense that our understanding and definition of God should continue to grow and evolve during our entire life and can never be complete.

When we look at the vast, physical universe surrounding us, we observe that there is an orderliness or consistency about it. Stand anywhere on the surface of our planet and you will find that gravity works in such a manner that if you drop an object from a height it will always fall down, never up. Similarly, if you plant a tomato seed, it will always develop into a tomato plant; never into a corn stalk or apple tree. This observable orderliness and consistency has provided the basis from which various scientific disciplines have been developed. These disciplines have allowed mankind to understand some of the workings of the universe and harness nature to do our

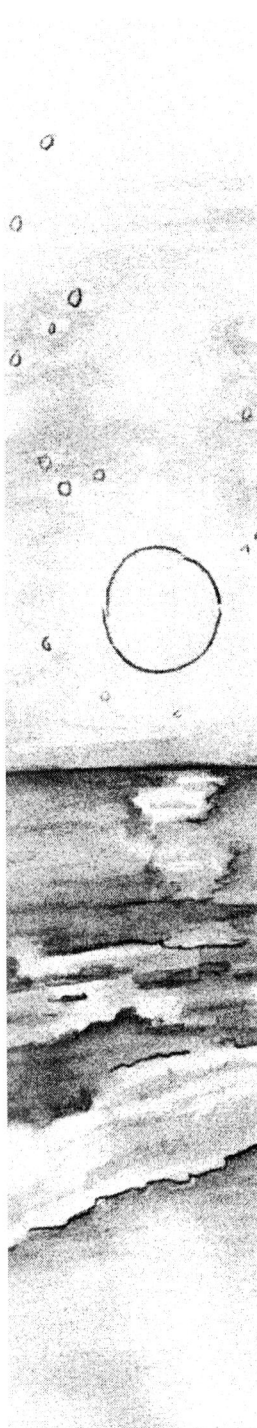

bidding. Science has given rise to modern conveniences such as plumbing, electricity, transportation, communication and so on. As time has progressed, so has our understanding of the workings of the universe. As such, scientific theories and hypotheses continue to be refined, developed, and evolve. Striving to understand how the universe works, via science, in no way precludes a belief in God. In fact, as we learn more about the detailed functioning of the universe, it serves to instill an ever-expanding sense of awe in how incredible the universe is, whether you believe in God or not. Once again, science does not conflict with a belief in God! If you do believe in God, science simply points to how awesome God is.

We all agree the Universe exists. It's an observable part of our life experience. Furthermore, it came from somewhere, was created at some time, in some manner, and by some thing or process. The question becomes was there, and is there, a consciousness to that which created the universe, and all that drives it along? If you say "yes" there is a consciousness, a presence, a sentience that created the universe with intention, then you would fit the definition of a person of faith. Similarly, if you feel that there is or was no consciousness driving the creation of the universe and all of its intricacies, and there is no presence, then you fit the definition of an atheist. In a sense, both types of people believe in a God. The difference is that one is a God of existence and the other is a God of non-existence. Either belief requires a strong faith, since there is, as of yet, no physical means to prove either belief to be correct. It's a personal choice we all make. In fact, it probably requires a slightly stronger faith to believe that this vast universe and all its intricacies could have been created without intention. Thus, contrary to popular belief, an atheist is not a person without faith, but rather one of tremendous faith.

So which one is right? Perhaps, in a way, both views are correct. As our awareness expands we begin to realize that it is very rare indeed that things are truly either black or white. Usually, there is a whole spectrum (not just shades of grey, but colors as well) between two apparent extremes. In Judeo-Christian scriptures it is said, "It is done unto you as you believe." A more detailed elaboration can be found in *The Science of Mind* by Ernest Holmes:

> Hence, it follows that if we believe that It (God) will not work, It really works by appearing to "not work." When we believe that It cannot and will not, then, according to the principle, It Does Not. But when It does not, It still does–only It does according to our belief that It will not.

In other words, it would appear that our beliefs shape our perceptions. We see similar phenomena in the quantum physical world, wherein the presence of the observer (the act of observation) affects the behavior of that which is being observed. Thus, it probably shouldn't be too surprising that this type of behavior also occurs on a macroscopic or even cosmic scale. So, it comes down to this: if you believe in God, the universe will provide ample evidence to confirm and support this belief. Similarly, if you don't believe in God, the universe will provide ample evidence to confirm your belief that God doesn't exist. In other words, it's a choice each of us gets to make and the corresponding experience will tend to confirm that choice.

For me, I definitely believe in God, and my perceptions and understanding of how God works continues to evolve as I experience life and journey down my spiritual path. In part, my belief stems from the fact that I find it hard to fathom how this awesome universe could have come into existence without intention. More importantly, however, as I have courted the divine over the years, and my relationship with God has grown, I have sensed Its presence. It has become a consistent part of my life and the more I focus on It the more I sense It. Thus, for me there is no denying that a God of consciousness is real. I feel that I have reached a stage wherein my belief is transcending into knowing. There is something far grander than my mind or ego, something that connects all of us, is in all of us, and is part and parcel of everything. This I call God. It is good and I am grateful. So, what is your choice?

Spirituality and Religion

Spirituality is
God's essence,
Religion is
Man's
interpretation

We are all spiritual beings having human experiences. Each of us has an innate desire to become aware of, and develop a connection to, God. In other words, we are predisposed to awaken to our spiritual nature. This awakening process I call spirituality. There are many paths which one can follow, which I call spiritual faith traditions. During our lives some of us do awaken to varying degrees and some of us do not. In addition, as human beings we have all been blessed with the gift of free will. Hence, the degree to which we choose to awaken is one of many choices we get to make in this life experience, which is all good!

I believe that religion is also a path to awakening. Religion is a man-made institution that originated from spirituality. As such, institutionalization tends to be accompanied by various human elements such as ego, control, power, politics and judgment. These human elements have a tendency to serve as a distraction, and can dilute the purity of the original spirituality-based intention. This is not to say religion is bad or inferior, but to point to the idea that the differences between religion and spirituality are often a major source of discomfort and disenfranchisement for many folks. Most folks who say they are uncomfortable with the "G word" probably don't have as much of an issue with God as they do with the image of God that many religions espouse. For this reason I think it is useful to examine some of the differences between spirituality and religion in various areas. I have observed and experienced the following:

Separation: Spirituality recognizes that God created the Universe from itself and is everywhere in all things including us. Thus, we are all connected, we are all one. Furthermore, each of us has the capacity to feel God's presence and have an intimate relationship with God. We were given the gift of free will to experience everything, including God's presence, as we desire. In contrast, religion recognizes that God created the universe, but also has a tendency to portray God as a distant entity, somehow separate from us. Religion often teaches that one needs an intermediary such as a priest or minister in order to gain God's favor. This illusion of separation and the failure to recognize that we are all one can perpetuate feelings of isolation not only from God but from other people as well.

Past, Present & Future: Spirituality recognizes the wisdom of the past and embraces the truth contained in ancient texts and scriptures, however it is focused on the present and living in the now. Heaven and Hell are viewed as states of consciousness that we experience now in this moment. God is always communicating; all we have to do is listen. In contrast, religion tends to be very much focused on the past and future. There tends to be considerable reverence in regard to ancient scriptures as "the" guide for attaining future salvation. Heaven and Hell are often depicted as geographical locations and afterlife destinations. Religion often conveys an impression that once the "holy book" was written, God stopped communicating. It is as if God said, "Well, that's all I've got to say, you're on your own kids!"

Love vs. Fear: Spirituality recognizes that God's nature is Love, and that God is always trying to gently direct us toward our greater good. As such, our nature is love as well, and we gravitate toward peace, harmony and helpfulness. All that we are is God and yet God is still much more. Religion, on the other hand, often portrays God as a judging deity, ruling on high and waiting to smite us as soon as we step out of line. Many religions teach that we need to be fearful of God. This atmosphere of fear is often used to coerce folks into behaving a certain way so as to avoid punishment or eternal damnation. Religion also tends to not trust people to do the right thing if left to their own devices. This brings to mind the words of Lau Tzu, from the Tao Te Ching, "If you don't trust people, you make them untrustworthy."

Many Paths: Spirituality recognizes that all faith traditions are valid, and that there are many paths to God. The world is a large place, filled with many people, all of whom are unique. Thus, it is extremely unlikely that any one path is going to be a good fit for everybody. A specific religion, on the other hand, often views its way as the only way, the only true path to God. There seems to be an elitist, exclusory attitude that there is one and only one path to salvation and all others lead to damnation. This attitude is often riddled with judgment and fear.

Tradition: Spirituality recognizes and embraces the utility of rituals and prayers. However, it is the intent and attitude behind the steps of the ritual and words of a prayer that are important, not the steps and words themselves. Similarly, spirituality recognizes and reveres wisdom contained in ancient text and scriptures, yet it is the truth that is important, not the vehicle that delivers this truth. In contrast, religion tends to place much emphasis and importance on performing rituals with precision, and reciting scripture and specific prayers verbatim. This indicates that the words and steps are more important than the intent or attitude or perhaps that the original intent has been forgotten.

I believe that both spirituality and religion can be a means to awakening, or paths to God. Furthermore, I think it is important to recognize that we are all unique individuals and each of us must search to find a path that is a good fit. Often, if we allow ourselves to be open and receptive, this path finds us. Recognize also that as our lives unfold, we are likely to find the paths that do work for us change as our consciousness expands.

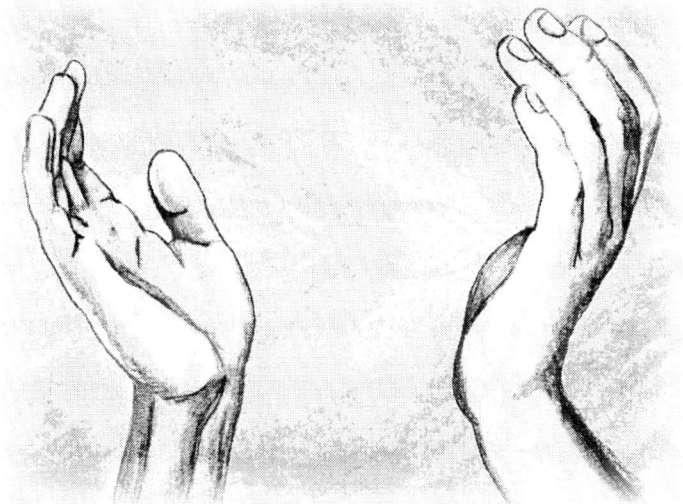

Science
and
Religion

It's not a question of choosing
between God and Science,
rather, it's about recognizing
that God is Science.

Many people today have strongly attached themselves to the false belief that science and spirituality, or science and religion, are somehow mutually exclusive. The fact is, science and spirituality are complimentary, and science and religion can be. Since God created the universe from Itself, and is everywhere in everything, this obviously includes science as well. God is science and so much more, and science is but a tool that mankind has developed in order to gain an understanding of some of the workings of God's awesome universe. I once heard it said, and unfortunately I don't remember by whom, "When we ask questions about the universe, the questions usually fall into one of two categories, why and how? Science points us in the direction of answering the how, and spirituality points us in the direction of answering the why."

Religions tend to rely quite heavily upon ancient scriptures and religious texts as guides for life. Much of the perceived disagreement or apparent contradiction between science and religion stems from literal, and often superficial, interpretations of these ancient writings. There are several compelling arguments that suggest that interpreting ancient scriptures literally, at face value, to be folly and of limited value.

Lost in Translation: Mainstream religious texts, such as the Torah, Bible and Koran, were not originally written in English. Some have been translated multiple times from one language to another and to another and so on. Anybody who speaks multiple languages, or has studied a foreign language, can attest to the fact that you cannot translate things exactly from one language to another. There's always a little something lost or changed when translating.

Change over time: Even within a given language the meaning of words and expressions changes over time. Just compare the parlance used in classic literature from the 19th or early 20th century to that used today and this becomes quite obvious. As a timely example, while I'm writing this chapter it

happens to be the holiday season and my children are singing Deck the Halls in the background. The lyric "don we now our gay apparel" jumps out as a case in point. Back when this song was written the word gay was most often used in the context of happy and festive. Today, gay is most often used in the context of homosexuality. Same word, same language, much different meaning. Ironically, I have a couple of close friends who have impeccable fashion sense and also happen to be gay. So from this context "gay apparel" could also be interpreted as meaning finest apparel. You get the point.

Parables: For many of the cultures affiliated with the writing of various scriptures, parable has always played a major role in their story telling, and communication of wisdom and history. Parables are typically fictional accounts yet they embody truth. For example, we may never know if there was really "a boy who cried wolf" but the unequivocal truth is if you sound enough false alarms, folks will eventually stop paying attention. Many scriptural stories are parable in nature. Hence, they may be fictional accounts that embody truth.

Words have their limits: Most ancient scriptures and religious texts were originally written by people who were divinely inspired. I too have felt divinely inspired to write at times, and I'm certain that I'm not the only person to find words woefully inadequate in conveying all that I'm thinking and feeling. This is especially true when the topics are rather abstract, as matters involving God tend to be.

So, if you take into account the facts that ancient scriptures have been translated multiple times, were written long ago, contain much in the way of parable, and words can be limiting, you don't have to be a rocket scientist to realize you can't place too much stock in literal, face value interpretations of scriptures. This is not to say that scriptures don't contain truth, they certainly do, only you must delve beneath the surface to truly get to it. For example, maybe Adam and Eve weren't two people per se, but rather a metaphor for a certain stage in human evolution, a turning point in human self-awareness and consciousness.

Once you let go of literal interpretations of scriptures and keep open to the idea that interpretations may be incomplete or inaccurate, contradictions with science evaporate. Similarly, one needs to remember that scientific theories are subject to revision as mankind learns more. As a species we have learned much but it is still only a minute fraction of all there is to know.

Setting the Fossil Record Straight

*Jesus and Darwin
are the best of friends*

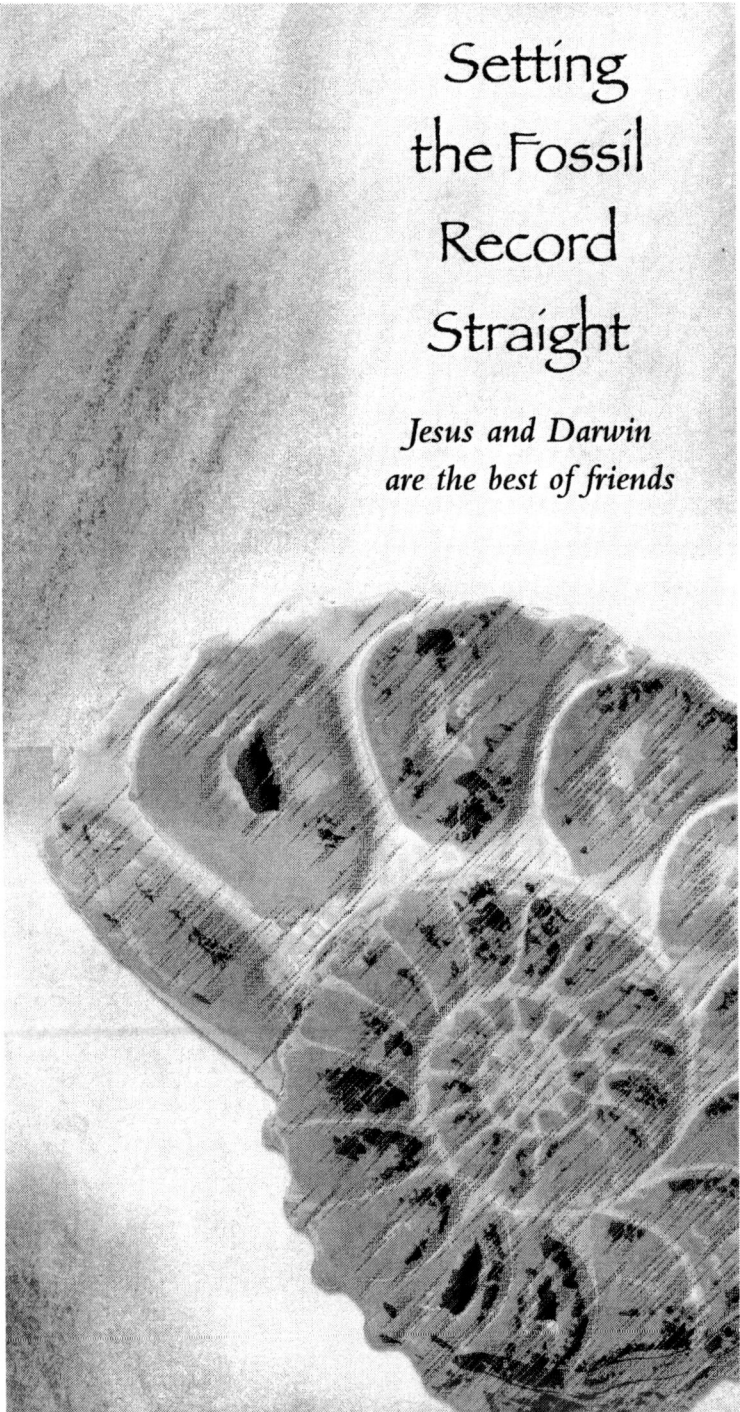

One scientific concept that the general public seems to have a great deal of misunderstanding about is the theory of evolution. There have been numerous occasions in recent years where I've listened to people passionately express their disbelief in evolution, and suggest that we should not teach the subject in public schools or at least we should teach alternative views such as "intelligent design." What amazes me is that most of these folks appear to be completely ignorant in their understanding of evolution, yet they feel so passionately about it being false or somehow conflicting with their belief in God or their religious teachings. I wonder if they were to actually take an introductory anthropology course, and really gain a true understanding of the subject, would they have a markedly different opinion? I believe the answer would be yes. Ignorance often seems to be the basis for most misunderstanding. So, my intention here is to clear up some of the misunderstandings I've encountered regarding evolution. I'd like to set the fossil record straight, and suggest that the theory of evolution in no way contradicts a belief in the existence of God. In fact, like all facets of science it paints an even grander picture of some of the detailed workings of this amazing universe that God created.

What is Evolution?

There is an abundance of geological and paleontological (fossil) evidence that suggests our planet has changed dramatically since its formation, and in the process so have the life forms inhabiting it. In general, life has become more sophisticated and diverse over time, thus better enabling life to adapt to environmental changes and hence survive. Evolution, in essence, is just a statement of this observation. In its simplest definition, the theory of evolution boils down to this: life changes over time, and it does so in response to environmental changes. What exactly drives this process has been a popular topic of study since the 19th century, and one of the most popular explanations is Darwin's principle of natural selection. According to this principle, life forms that are successful in adapting to changes in their environment survive, and those that are unsuccessful perish and become extinct. Understanding how life forms are able to adapt to environmental changes is a goal of such scientific disciplines as physiology, genetics and epigenetics. Although details to the mechanisms driving the process of evolution (in other words how evolution works) continue to be refined, the simple truth remains: life does change over time, and it seemingly does so in response to environmental changes.

Are we descended from Monkeys?

One popular misconception is the belief that the theory of evolution suggests that humans are descended from monkeys. This is incorrect. As mentioned previously all that the theory of evolution suggests is that life changes over time, and it does so in response to environmental changes. Two scientific disciplines that embrace the theory of evolution, and seek to understand the ancestor/descendant relationships of life forms on Earth are paleontology and anthropology. The science of paleontology seeks to understand the history of all life on Earth by examining fossilized remains. The science of anthropology is very similar, but is more focused on the history of life as it relates to human beings. According to paleontology and anthropology, the fossil record overwhelmingly suggests that all life forms that exist on Earth today are branches of a vast family tree that can be traced back to the first primitive or primordial life form that existed on this planet several billion years ago. As with any family tree some branches share common ancestors more recently than others. The term "common ancestor" refers to the original pair or group of creatures whose offspring gave rise to new species.

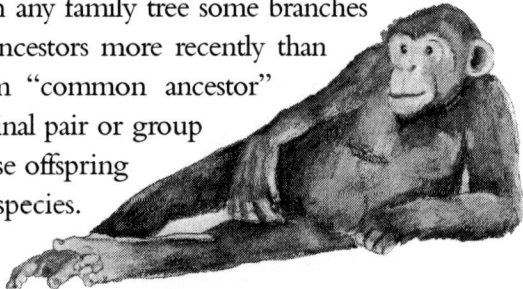

Paleontologists and anthropologists theorize that if you compare all of the life forms that exist today, physically and genetically, creatures that are similar to one another share a common ancestor more recently in time than creatures that are dissimilar. For example: humans are more similar both physically and genetically to monkeys than they are to dogs. Thus, it is believed that humans and monkeys share a common ancestor more recently in time than humans and dogs. Similarly, humans and dogs share a common ancestor more recently in time than humans and spiders, and humans and spiders share a common ancestor more recently in time than humans and redwood trees. Comparative studies such as this enable the scientific community to determine relative branching points (i.e. this one occurred before that one) in the family tree, but in order to estimate when these branching points actually occurred, and what the ancestral creatures might have looked like, one must refer to the fossil record. Anthropology actually theorizes that humans and monkeys descended from a common ancestor, not that humans descended from monkeys.

The Fossil Record

A second area of misconception is the fossil record. As an aside, my teenage son sometimes jokingly refers to some of the music I listen to as dinosaur rock. So, for his benefit, and those of his age group, let me clarify that the fossil record that I am referring to here is not one of my Led Zeppelin albums. Many folks wonder what is this fossil record? Where do fossils come from? How do geologists determine how old fossils are, and so on? To answer these questions, we must briefly discuss some background information. Welcome to my abbreviated version of Geology 101. Ever since our Earth was very young, floods have deposited dirt, mud, and rocks onto flood plains, rivers have transported and deposited materials into lake basins and upon ocean floors, and volcanoes have spewed forth ash, rocks, and lava depositing them in similar locations. As a result, many places on earth have sedimentary soils and rocks that resemble a layer cake with the younger layers typically at the top and the older layers at depth. In addition, animal remains occasionally get incorporated into the layers and if conditions like soil type, moisture content, temperature, and ph are just right, fossilization occurs. That is, a chemical process takes place that transforms bone, teeth and shell into stone, thus preserving a record of an animal's existence.

What is interesting and useful about volcanic deposits is that they often contain radioisotopes, which are unstable radioactive variants of certain elements. Carbon-14 and uranium-238 are common examples. These isotopes break down into stable, non-radioactive elements and they do so at consistent, predictable rates. For example, carbon-14 breaks down into nitrogen-14 and has a half-life of 5730 years. That is, the amount of carbon-14 in a volcanic deposit will reduce by half every 5730 years. Without going into excessive detail, you can essentially measure the amount of the radioisotope and the amount of its decay product in a volcanic deposit, and by knowing the rate of the decay you can determine how long it's been decaying. Hence, you can determine when the deposit was first formed. In essence, each volcanic layer provides a time benchmark to which you can relate the ages of neighboring fossils.

In addition, the surface of our planet is essentially a collection of relatively thin plates, and these plates tend to gradually move about over time, driven by internal geological processes. This is a simplified description of plate tectonic theory. One of the consequences of tectonic movement is that some areas that were once ocean floor or lakebeds can be forced upward or "uplifted" to elevations above sea level. Weathering and erosional processes then gradually carve away and expose these uplifted sedimentary layers and some of the fossils contained within. The Grand Canyon is a great example. As you descend into the Canyon you are effectively going back in time. Fossils at the bottom of the Canyon are typically much older than those near the top.

This cursory explanation of some geological processes is probably as detailed as the average person would care to read about, yet it gives you a rudimentary idea of how fossils form and how their age is determined. The main point to remember here is that there are well-established techniques based on decades of observation and experiment which enable geologists to determine with confidence when certain creatures graced the face of the earth, and what environmental conditions were like during that time. Conditions that lead to fossilization are rather specialized. Hence, the remains of most creatures do not become fossilized. Finding fossils is no easy task and the same weathering processes that reduce mountains to rubble can and do destroy fossils as well.

In essence, the fossil record is like a giant chronological jigsaw puzzle that depicts various life forms that have lived on our planet. What's particularly challenging is that many of the pieces are missing and there is no picture to show what the completed puzzle is supposed to look like. Thus, scientists arrange the pieces they have in a manner that makes the most logical sense, and when more pieces are found, they are incorporated into the puzzle and readjustments are made as necessary. In short, the fossil record is a work in progress.

We are all Relatives, We are One!

Using the anthropology approach let's consider the following. You and your siblings share a common ancestor, your

parents. Similarly, you and your first cousins share a common ancestor, your grandparents. With your second cousins the common ancestor would be your great-grandparents. As you progress back through time, generation by generation, you begin to realize that you are related in a progressively more distant manner to folks in your community, your state, your country, and the world. In short, this approach would suggest that if you go back far enough in time, you would find that all humans came from a common ancestor. Perhaps you'd like to call this common ancestor Adam and Eve. You can continue back further in time and find a common ancestor for all primates (which includes humans), mammals, etc. All life can be traced back to a common ancestor. Ironically, when we strip away all of the misunderstanding, we find that scientific disciplines profess what is embraced by most faith traditions: we are all relatives, we are one!

Reconciling Creationism and Evolution

All of the great enlightened mystical teachers that have graced the earth throughout history have recognized the principle of Unity. From this principle comes the profound realization that the Divine is the source and substance of everything, both animate and inanimate, and every situation and circumstance. The Divine expresses and experiences Itself uniquely through and as all of Its creations. Thus, in its simplest of terms, life can be defined as the play of God awakening to Itself through and as all of Its created forms. In essence the universe is a playground for God to experience and express Its infinite nature. Given that God is also eternal; it makes perfect sense that God created a universe that is dynamic, ever-changing, and hence ever-evolving. If this were not true, the experiential potential that the universe has to offer would soon be exhausted and life would become monotonous, repetitive and pointless.

The only conflict that exists between creationism and evolutionary theory is when folks get attached to literal interpretations of the stories of creationism, such as Genesis. As inferred in chapter eight, as we as a society mature and begin to interpret such ancient stories from metaphorical, symbolic and metaphysical points of view, we find that all contradiction dissolves. Evolution simply becomes a process within the larger process of creation, and feelings of conflict are replaced by feelings of awe and reverence for the amazing universe in which we live. A universe that is fueled by, and created in the image and likeness of, its Ineffable Source.

It's worth repeating that ignorance often is the basis for misunderstanding. Of course, if left unchecked, ignorance can lead to false assumptions, fear, hate and violence. If folks simply take the time to learn about subjects, people, and cultures that they know little about, they can avoid developing strong, unfounded, negative feelings towards that about which they are ignorant. This, I believe, is an essential step to becoming a peaceful inhabitant in the world.

3 Insights

*Life can
be as difficult
or easy as we
choose it to be.
Each of us is
endowed with the
ability to be a
conscious co-creator
of our destiny,
the architect
of our experience.*

Letter
to
Friend

*Life is an unending
series of choices
and results.*

A friend of mine and her mother had a falling out and didn't speak to each other for over 20 years. Then, about five years ago, they reconnected and sort of buried the hatchet. Thankfully it was in a place other than each other's skull. Yet, there remained much in the way of unresolved baggage and recently they've had another falling out. This friend of mine is a wonderful person, yet she is very attached to her story, her past. As such she remains a victim of life rather than a participant or a co-creator. After receiving correspondences from both her and her mother, I found myself hearing it from both sides in a role not unlike a counselor. I decided to offer some thoughts and perspectives that I hoped would be useful, while remaining supportive, loving and neutral. Here is the letter I sent.

Dear Friend:

So sorry to hear about your current falling out. The good news is that with every falling out the stage is set for an even closer and more meaningful falling in. Every relationship has its unique collection of experiences and the resulting emotions, ups and downs, and history. Not having walked a mile in either of your shoes, I cannot truly know or fully grasp your story. I can, however, offer some thoughts and perspectives you might find useful and comforting.

In Buddhism it is said, "Attachment is the root of all suffering." This can include attachment to the story of our lives. We all have experiences that we look back upon and we find ourselves saying things like "I wish I could do that over again" or "I wish this had happened instead of that." This brings to mind a quote from The Rubaiyat *by Omar Khayyam: "The moving finger writes, and having writ, moves on: nor all your piety nor wit shall lure it back to cancel half a line, nor all your tears wash out a word of it." The point being, of course, there is no changing or rewriting the past; so let it go and you'll be happier for it. All we can do is draw wisdom from the past, bless it and move on.*

In our society, we are taught to look at the story of our lives and judge it. We call this experience "good" and that one "bad." We call this choice "right" and that one "wrong." The mystical teachers, philosophers, sages and gurus over the millennia have suggested a different approach. Rather than judge our past, simply recognize it as a series of choices and results that are neither bad nor good. It's all cause and effect. As Shakespeare said "Nothing is either bad or good, but that our thinking makes it so." We would do well to simply honor our past experiences and recognize that they have helped bring us to where we are and who we are today. The real question is what are we going to do from this point forward?

The reality you experience today is the result of yesterday's thoughts, and tomorrow is being shaped by what you are dwelling upon right now. Our chronic way of thinking, our beliefs, create our reality. This has been recognized for thousands of years. In Buddhism it is said, "Show me what you dwell upon, and I'll show you who you are." In Christianity it is said, "It is done unto you as you believe" and "As you sew, so shall you reap." Philosophers and spiritual teachers recognize this truth and also that if we remain anchored to the past we continue to recreate the same sort of feelings time and again. The circumstances may vary but the feelings are all too familiar. Yet, each of us has the power to write our life story from this point in time forward however we wish it to be. How you might ask? I know of two keys: forgiveness and gratitude.

In other words, forgiveness is getting to the point where one can surrender the past and let it go gracefully, without attachment. Another definition of forgiveness is allowing one that we begrudged, disliked, etc. (notice the past tense) safe passage in our minds. During the course of our lives we all experience situations where folks make choices that hurt us or upset us and we find ourselves completely justified in our resentment, dislike, or condemnation towards this person. We then ask, "Why should I forgive them? I'm totally justified in feeling this way!" The answer is "Yes, you are, but you are the one who wants the healing." True healing cannot occur until we forgive. As Jesus said "Forgive us our trespasses and those that trespass against us." We need to forgive ourselves in addition to other folks. Unforgiveness keeps us anchored in the past and only harms us. I think Michael Beckwith said it best: *"Unforgiveness is like taking poison in hopes that it harms the other person."* As long as one holds on to unforgiveness one remains a victim. Forgiveness is the key to breaking the bonds of victimization.

A good way to diffuse negative thinking and reshape your thoughts is through gratitude. Every time you find yourself brooding about some past experience (whether it happened yesterday or 40 years ago) or something current that pisses you off, stop and take a deep breath, and gently turn your focus toward the things in your life for which you are grateful. For example, the scent of a rose in bloom, the colors of the sky during sunset, the taste of your favorite foods, being alive, being able to walk, having all your faculties functioning, the joy of friendship, songs that resonate with you, and so on. What you will notice is that you will start feeling uplifted, your mood will shift and gradually you will find more things that bring about feelings of gratitude. Things you are grateful for will begin to manifest increasingly in your life. As you sew so shall you reap!

Ultimately what happens in life is irrelevant; it's who you are while you're alive that is important. As humans we are blessed with the gift of free will. We are the authors and we get to choose where the story of our lives goes from this point forward. What is your next chapter going to look like?

Here is a Native American saying that I find very profound: *"Take everything in the palms of your hands and see what's worth keeping, then blow the rest away with a breath of kindness. Hold on to what works and throw away what doesn't work for you. Enjoy every day of life that you have been given and be thankful for it."*

I hope you find these words useful.

Peace & Love,

CJ

The mother seemed to grasp what I was saying. Whether or not any of it gets put into practice only time will tell, yet, awareness is always the first step. Sadly, my friend didn't seem to get it at all. She is still attached to the role of victim and believes that her healing and happiness are dependent upon the actions and reactions of others. My good friend and spiritual mentor, Rev. Dr. David Bruner, once told me "There is one thing that most folks will do anything to avoid. They will give up their happiness, their health, their money, their relationships, even their lives to avoid this one thing. And, that one thing is to change!" Even when loved ones are habitually making choices that bring upset, drama, disappointment, or misery into their lives, we would do well to avoid judging them, their choices and the results. Remember that folks change if and only if they choose to change. Despite what our egos would like for us to believe, we can't force anyone to change if they don't want to. So, love them, support them and if they are open to it or request it, offer advice and let it go. If they take it to heart, great; if not, let it go, you've done all you can do. Remember that they too were given the gift of freewill and get to experience the results of their choices. Once again I'm reminded of the simple wisdom in the old saying "You can lead a horse to water, but you can't make him (or her) drink it."

A definition of forgiveness that I find profound is:
Forgiveness is abandoning all hope of a better past.

Health
and
Healing

*Often we
focus too much
on symptoms
and not enough
on root causes*

The human body has a remarkable, innate healing capacity. When confronted with injury, illness or disease it is naturally designed to initiate various physiological responses to return it to a state of optimal health. Thus, our natural or default state is one of vibrant health. Of course, some injuries are seemingly beyond our body's ability to repair completely. Fortunately, we are blessed to be living in an age where modern medicine has developed an amazing array of repair techniques and procedures. For example, arthroscopic and laparoscopic surgical procedures have eliminated a majority of the collateral damage that used to result from much more invasive surgical procedures, producing better results and quicker recovery times. Similarly, LASIK eye surgery can alleviate various visual deficiencies with minimal side effects and recovery time. Knee and shoulder reconstruction, as well as hip and other joint replacement procedures, have enabled many folks to fully recover from injuries and degenerative conditions that not many years ago would have resulted in permanent disability and chronic pain. The list goes on and on, and there appears to be still more promising developments on the horizon with the advent of stem cell research.

Sometimes our healing capacity is diminished to the point where we end up contracting certain illnesses and we find that we are unable to recover completely, expediently or without complications from these conditions. For many of these situations, there are a variety of effective treatment options to help our bodies return to a healthier state. Of these treatment options, the pharmaceutical-based approach is by far the most common. However, alternatives such as herbal, holistic, chiropractic, acupuncture and energy medicines are gaining popularity and are quite effective for many situations. We are fortunate to be living in an age where we have so many options available to us; yet, having all of these treatment options can be both a blessing and a curse. As our society becomes more reliant on these treatment options, there is a tendency to focus on treating symptoms, rather than identifying and eliminating root causes to the illnesses and diseases that ail us. There is also a tendency to overmedicate, and for every ailment that we seemingly cure, there is soon another to replace it. Many if not most of the illnesses and diseases that plague our society such as heart disease, diabetes and cancer stem from a common root cause: our lifestyle. By lifestyle I am referring to the choices we make regarding: diet, exercise, sleep, and dealing with stress; plus our attitude and beliefs. I'll address each of these areas after I first discuss the pitfalls of overmedicating.

The Perils of Overmedicating

Many folks have forgotten that most medicines do not heal in and of themselves. Rather, they assist the body to heal itself, as it's naturally designed to do. Some medicines are essentially concentrated forms of chemical compounds that our bodies naturally produce on their own to affect the healing process. One complication that does occur when using this type of medication is the fact that our bodies tend to produce and deliver healing agents in a localized fashion, to wherever the ailment is specifically located. In contrast, when healing agents are delivered via medication, they are distributed throughout the entire body. Different parts or systems within our body often react differently to these healing agents. So, as Bruce Lipton points out in his book *The Biology of Belief*, side effects are

really effects. As an example, an individual starts taking a certain medication to treat a particular ailment, but soon this person has a whole pharmacy within his or her medicine cabinet to treat all of the various so-called "side effects." Hence the old adage, "sometimes the treatment is worse than the disease." If such an individual were to simply address the root cause to his or her ailment, perhaps they would require no medications whatsoever.

Other types of medicines are designed to stimulate our bodies to produce higher levels of desired healing agents. While elevated levels may appear to initially speed or aid the healing process, they are not without complication. One such complication that often occurs is that the feedback mechanism that our body would normally rely upon to determine if it needs to increase or decrease production of a healing agent gets messed up. As a result, our body's ability to auto-regulate how much healing agent it produces becomes impaired. Consequently, once the treatment is stopped there tends to be a recovery period when the body struggles to stabilize and normalize its feedback and regulating mechanisms. This type of complication is not uncommon for medicines that are designed to adjust or alter body chemistry, especially brain chemistry.

Antibiotics are a family of medications that have, justifiably, received praise for their ability to treat many bacterial infections. However, there has been growing concern about the tendency to over prescribe and improperly use these medications and how this contributes to the development of resistant strains of bacteria. In addition, most antibiotics are indiscriminant in the bacteria that they kill. While very effective in eliminating the bacteria causing, for example, an ear infection or strep throat, antibiotics also kill beneficial bacteria, such as that which aids our digestion. When treatment is complete, there is an additional recovery period before our bodies return to normal and are fully healed.

Our society has a growing tendency to focus on symptoms rather than root causes. The most dire consequence with this approach is that treating symptoms rarely if ever cures a disease. You may succeed in masking it or suppressing it for a while, but it is likely to either resurface or manifest in other ways. Sadly, it's all too common to hear of an individual who contracts a form of cancer, goes through the whole chemotherapy and radiation regimen to eliminate the cancer, returns to their pre-cancer lifestyle only to contract the disease again and die from it. Obviously, treating symptoms is only a temporary fix; it is not a cure. For complete healing to occur, the root cause of a disease must be addressed. Our lifestyle choices regarding diet, exercise, sleep, dealing with stress, our attitude and beliefs are the root cause for many ailments. Most ailments are simply a wake-up call to get our attention so that we realize that our lives are out of balance in some manner.

Lifestyle Factors

Diet & Exercise: For our bodies to have all that they need to perform all of their metabolic activities, and to function optimally, good hydration and a balanced diet is essential. Such a diet includes an abundant variety of fresh vegetables and fruits; is low in fat and processed sugar; comprises foods that are minimally processed and contain minimal chemical additives, preservatives and artificial ingredients; and is more plant-based and less animal-based. In addition, organic products are preferable and beneficial in that the absence of pesticide residues makes digesting these food items less taxing on the filtering organs of the body. The type, quantity and quality of food we consume certainly affects our susceptibility to illness and disease, and contributes to conditions such as obesity and hypertension.

Most folks are well aware that consistent exercise can have multiple health benefits. Engaging in frequent physical activity is good for toning and conditioning our bodies, which allows them to function more efficiently. Exercise is known to cause our bodies to produce endorphins which make us feel good. Consistent exercise slows the rate of decline in physical ability that typically accompanies aging.

In addition, exercise is a very effective means to relive stress. Usually, when you are working out you tend to be more focused on the "now" (i.e. fully engaged in your work out) as opposed to dwelling in the past or obsessing about the future. It brings you back to a state of human "being" and not human "doing." A word of caution though. This potential benefit can be compromised for folks who prefer to have some distraction (i.e. watching TV or listening to the radio) while working out. Distraction, by its very nature, takes you out of being in the now. If this is your preference and you are not yet ready to give it up, I would strongly suggest that you at least avoid watching or listening to the news or political talk shows or anything that creates negative feelings. As we shall soon see, negative feelings can undermine our health. If your work out is such that you feel you need distraction, music is a wonderful option. Otherwise consider finding a form of exercise that you find more enjoyable. Diet and exercise are wonderful ways in which we can honor our body temple.

Sleep: Our bodies are most active and effective in performing their healing and repair functions while we sleep. Getting a consistent and restful night's sleep has a significant impact on our state of health and our healing capacity. Disruptions to our sleep patterns not only can make us irritable, but can also make us more vulnerable to illness and disease.

As a father of four children I've gone through many cycles where the demands of parenthood have caused prolonged disruptions to my sleep patterns and inconsistency with

my exercise routines. Typically, I very rarely catch a cold or flu, yet each time I go through one of these cycles, my frequency of getting sick has increased noticeably. Of course my exposure to viruses increases dramatically via my children being in play groups, pre-school and school, yet if I get consistent exercise and sleep I'm usually quite successful in not contracting any of the illnesses caused by these viruses.

Stress: Numerous clinical studies have shown conclusively that elevated stress levels can suppress immune system response. This can make us more vulnerable to illness and disease. How we deal with prolonged periods of stress can have a profound effect on our health, and learning how to cope with stress effectively is paramount in maintaining optimum health and well being. There are many ways to alleviate stress: exercise, meditation, yoga, tai chi, spiritual practice, and going for walks in nature. Even sex can be an effective way to relive stress. Basically, anything that snaps you out of "doing" mode and into "being" mode and assuages any fears that may have captured your attention is a wonderful way to reduce stress.

Buddhism
"Show me what you dwell upon and I'll show you who you are."

Judeo-Christian
"It is done unto you as you believe."

Gandhi
"Your beliefs become your thoughts, your thoughts become your words, your words become your actions, your actions become your habits, your habits become your values, your values become your destiny."

Stress is rooted in fear, and often in the form of worry. Interestingly, when you worry about an undesirable future occurrence, you begin to engage the same emotional and physiological responses you'd experience if the event were to actually occur. So in a very real sense you truly experience that which you worry about, simply by virtue of worrying regardless of whether or not the event comes to pass. Thus, unlearning the habit of worrying is a very effective way to reduce stress. This brings to mind the upbeat, dare I say infectious (after all this chapter is about health and healing) lyrics by Bobby McFerrin, "Don't worry, be happy." Find a collection of ways to alleviate stress that work for you and do them consistently. You will likely be healthier and happier as a result.

Attitude and Beliefs: Thoughts that are positive, constructive and empowering serve to strengthen our healing capacity. Thoughts that are negative, destructive and draining tend to weaken our healing capacity. In other words, a positive attitude towards life and oneself, a positive self image, helps make us more resistant to disease, and a negative attitude makes us more susceptible to disease. I have not developed an ability to simply think away all illness, and that's not what I'm suggesting. In time, however, human consciousness is almost certain to evolve to the point where we can tap into the enormous healing potential of the mind, which is likely to be orders of magnitude more powerful than any drug. Let's take a closer look at how attitude and our underlying belief system affect our healing capacity.

Thoughts are the genesis of creativity. Every man-made object you see began as a thought in some human's mind. Yet, not every thought you entertain will manifest before your eyes, which is a good thing since we have so many, disparate, often conflicting thoughts on any given day. Rather, the environment of your thinking, or the chronic way in which you think (which is a product of your conscious and subconscious belief system) is what manifests the reality that you experience. It's true! Philosophers and spiritual teachers have espoused this wisdom for thousands of years. Once again in Buddhism it is said, "Show me what you dwell upon and I'll show you who you are." In Judeo-Christian scripture it is said, "It is done unto you as you believe." More recently Gandhi said, "Your beliefs become your thoughts, your thoughts become your words, your words become your actions, your actions become your habits, your habits become your values, your values become your destiny." In other words, you create your life experience by the thoughts you dwell upon which are a product of your belief system. Your health is but one facet of your life experience, and your thoughts most certainly do affect your health and your healing capacity.

Consider the placebo effect. Every year pharmaceutical companies run clinical trials for new medications, and in the process they always have a control group to which they give a placebo. Often the healing rate in the control group is comparable to that of the medicated group. This obviously begs the question: what then is really driving the healing, is it the drug, or is it the mind via belief in the drug's effectiveness? The effectiveness of a treatment or a doctor has been shown to be directly related to a patient's belief in the treatment or doctor. Likewise, the likelihood of contracting a disease or health issue has been shown to be directly related to a person's belief in their susceptibility or predisposition for such conditions. Clearly the mind has a very powerful influence on both creating and healing disease. However, western medicine is only beginning to understand, appreciate and tap into this resource. Pioneering physicians such as Larry Dossey, Bernie Siegel, Carl Simonton, Lawrence LaShan, Mamet Oz, Elson Haas, Herbert Benson, and Andrew Weil are among some of those who have broken ranks with the traditional pharmaceutical based (and sponsored) approaches to healing. Their exploration of alternative healing modalities and efforts to bring them into western mainstream is proving to be effective and encouraging, yet it's just the beginning.

Of the lifestyle choices discussed above, diet, exercise and sleep are probably the easiest to adjust; developing an effective way to deal with stress is probably a little more challenging; and, changing one's attitude and underlying beliefs is the most challenging. Most folks move through life unaware that the majority of their reactions and responses are a product of the mainstream or societal belief system that has been programmed into their subconscious minds and hardwired into their neural pathways since they were born. They are unaware that some of the beliefs that were taught to them are either untrue or are a misinterpretation of truth. They often don't realize that they can consciously change these programs and rewire their neural pathways, if they desire, to something that better serves them. I know of two effective ways to do this, and I would imagine there are other ways as well.

Breaking the Cycle (making changes)

One approach is to examine the atmosphere of your thoughts by systematically looking at your beliefs as they pertain to your health and well being, and see how they are serving you. Begin by asking yourself some questions. For example, how do you feel about your body? Do you view it as a miraculous temple that houses your soul and enables you to engage the wondrous human experience? Do you view it as being full of potential to be developed as you choose? Do you view it as being worthy of your love and attention exactly as it is and exactly as it isn't? Or, conversely, do you judge your body harshly and deem it unworthy of love and respect until it conforms to a model that society dictates as perfect? Do you deem it flawed, problematic and something you are stuck with? As another example, how do you feel about the food you eat? Do you view it as a means to express love and gratitude toward your body temple? Do you view it as a wonderful simple pleasure in life that offers incredible variety and delicious experience? Do you view it as an opportunity to develop good habits, knowing that sometimes things that are good for us are an acquired taste? Or, do you view food and eating as a continuous, nagging compromise between good taste and good

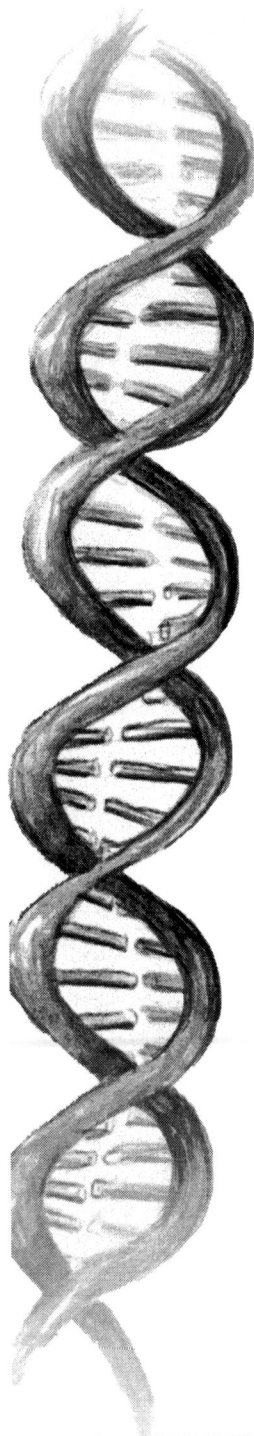

health, the source of many of your problems, and needing to conform to the latest diet trends? Answer questions such as these honestly, yet without judgment or attachment. See how they relate to your current state of health and well being. Consider also the lifestyle factors discussed previously, how do you feel about these? Keep in mind that feelings are indicative of underlying beliefs. Dig in and see what you discover. Where you find negative thoughts and beliefs, consider positive alternatives and keep in mind that a positive thought is known to be 100 times more powerful in its creative potential than a negative thought. Doing this, you are effectively weeding out the beliefs that are not serving you and replacing them with ones that do. This approach is definitely doable. However, it requires dedication and consistency to rewrite subconscious programs and it takes time. You must become aware so that you can recognize when you are reacting in one of your undesired programmed responses, stop yourself and say, "No more! I used to react that way, but not any more. Now I react this way." Eventually the new response will take root and the old will fade away.

Another way that works equally as well, is the spiritual approach. Clues to this approach can be found in Christian scripture where it is said "Seek first his kingdom... and all else shall be provided unto you." In addition, Jesus said "The kingdom of heaven lies within." These same ideas are echoed in other faith traditions. If you focus on cultivating your awareness of God, your consciousness of God, and your connection to God, then everything will naturally fall into place with relative ease. If you subscribe to the school of thought that we are spiritual beings having human experiences, this makes perfect sense. You realize that your spirit (soul, divine essence, call it what you will) is, in fact, God. As such, there is a part of you that is immortal, knows only perfect health, truth, love, and joy. Thus, each of us has an internal compass to guide us, and this trumps any false beliefs we may have picked up during our life's journey. I have had success with both approaches; however, I find the second approach to be less arduous and more enjoyable.

What about Genetics?

You might be thinking to yourself, "Ok, I can appreciate how lifestyle choices can affect my healing capacity, but what about genetics? What about folks who have a family history for a certain disease, and consequently envision their body to be a genetic time-bomb and that it is only a matter of time until some predestined disease surfaces? In some ways aren't we victims of our genes?" Once again, let me reiterate that I believe that human body is naturally programmed for optimal health. Furthermore, the overwhelming majority of folks are born with adequate genes to lead healthy, happy lives. For folks who subscribe to the genetic victim theory, here are some points to consider.

1 There is a distinct difference between causation and correlation. While it's true that there are some diseases (i.e. cystic fibrosis) that have been identified as being "caused" by the presence of a particular gene, there are far more ailments, such as heart disease, diabetes, and cancer, that are only "correlated" to the presence of particular genes. In these correlation cases some folks who posses the genes express the disease, and others do not. Thus, the presence of a particular gene or multiple genes seems to be related to certain diseases, but is not the sole cause.

2 Genes are effectively blueprints that cells use to produce protein molecules, which are some of the fundamental building blocks for life. Importantly, genes are not self-activating or self-emergent. They don't turn themselves on and off, nor do they produce proteins on their own volition. Rather, regulatory proteins, in response to environmental signals, determine which genes to access and ultimately what proteins to produce. In other words, using a construction analogy, genes are essentially the blueprints and regulatory proteins are the contractor. A contractor works from the blueprints but often has to improvise depending upon environmental factors.

3 A multitude of proteins can be produced from each gene. This was one of the big surprises from the human genome project conducted in the late 20th century. Initially, it was believed that each gene sequence was a code for one and only one protein. Since the human body produces something on the order of 120,000 different proteins, it was expected that when human DNA was completely mapped out it would be found to contain 120,000 genes. However, scientists were shocked to discover that human DNA contains roughly 25,000 genes. The fact that a single gene can be used to produce more than one protein explains why some folks with a particular gene develop a health condition while others do not.

4 Environmental signals that initiate and direct protein production can be physical, chemical or electromagnetic. Thoughts are known to be electromagnetic in nature. Hence, thoughts have the potential to

influence genetic expression. This, of course further substantiates the idea that our thoughts can affect our health.

Genes certainly play a significant role in some diseases, but more often than not they do so in conjunction with environmental factors. Lifestyle choices can profoundly affect our health, even for conditions that are "correlated" to the presence of certain genes.

To Summarize

The human body has an amazing healing capacity, and our body's default setting is one of optimal health. The effectiveness of our healing capacity is dependent on our lifestyle choices plus our attitude and beliefs. Specifically, these choices include eating a balanced and nutritious diet; getting consistent exercise and sleep; adopting effective ways to handle stress; and cultivating a positive life-affirming attitude and belief system. When we neglect these areas, we weaken our healing capacity and set the stage for contracting illness and disease. In fact, I strongly believe that this is the root cause for most of the ailments that afflict our society, such as heart disease, diabetes, cancer, hypertension, erectile dysfunction, obesity, high cholesterol, allergies, and more. If we simply make choices that promote good health and well being, it is very likely that we will not suffer from any of these ailments. This brings to mind the wisdom of the old saying, "an once of prevention is worth a pound of cure." Having said all of this, I realize that we are all human (at least in our incarnated form), and life has a way of happening such that despite our best intentions, we sometimes find ourselves ill and we need to make some lifestyle adjustments. Fortunately, we are living in an age where there are many effective treatment options to help us while we make these adjustments, but always remember treating symptoms will seldom cure the disease. Good luck and good health to you!

The Age of "Infotainment"

If it doesn't make your heart sing, why do it?

We are currently living in an era of "corporatized infotainment." That is, a small handful of individuals and corporations owning and controlling the overwhelming majority of our nation's mainstream media outlets, including newspapers, radio and television. These individuals and corporations have a disconcerting amount of control and influence as to what news stories are reported and how they are spun. Attracting as large an audience as possible, maintaining political affiliations, and perpetuating ideologies all come into play when such decisions are made. It is quite common for stories to be dramatized and sensationalized in order to capture people's attention. The news stories that we read, hear and see, and how they are presented, have much to do with what provides the most monetary and political benefit to the media ownership.

In addition, journalistic ethics and integrity seem to have disappeared. Prior to the Reagan administration, reporting news stories was similar to being under oath in a courtroom: substantiate your claims or face serious repercussions. Today, you can say just about anything, true or false, about anybody and there are few consequences or sincere efforts to set the record straight when distortions or flat-out lies are discovered. Listen to the disparate accounts between conservative and liberal oriented talk shows. For instance, if you compare reports by Rush Limbaugh and Ann Coulter to those by Ed Schultz and Randi Rhodes about events occurring on Capitol Hill, in Iraq, and so on, you will most likely hear completely contradictory accounts. Obviously they can't all be telling the truth. The irony is that we are living in the age of information, yet it is extremely difficult to know what information to believe. Opinion is packaged and sold as fact and often there are political or self-serving ulterior motives behind expressed opinions. Sadly, there is no longer a prevalent effort to disseminate unbiased factual information to the general public. The purpose of the free press in 21st century America is not simply the noble pursuit of informing and educating people, but rather to entertain them and generate profit.

Another aspect of the news that is particularly disturbing is the excessive focus on negativity. Despite all of the wonderful, positive things going on in our world, the majority of stories that actually get reported are to do with murder, death, destruction, and disasters. They say, "The news is news because it is the exception not the rule." So, what then of all the positive exceptions to the rule? Many folks believe that mainstream society isn't interested in positive stories, and these stories don't capture the attention of the masses. Centuries ago folks believed that the earth was flat and the earth was the center of the universe. Folks believed this because they were told it was the truth, but eventually they figured out that this was not the case. I wonder if the same situation exists with this belief that only negative stories sell? Most people I know dislike all of the negativity that is so pervasive in the news media. It paints a distorted inaccurate picture of a hopeless, chaotic world filled with thieves, murderers, and terrorists. Some folks think there is intention behind this continual diet of negativity in that people are more easily manipulated and controlled if they are kept in a state of fear and despair. Whatever the motives, rarely does reading, listening to, or watching the news leave you feeling happy, encouraged, or empowered. Rather, it quite often leaves you feeling upset, disheartened, powerless and angry. Since your attitude affects your state of being, limiting your exposure to this type of negative input would be wise. If the news doesn't make your heart sing, avoid it.

As an example, I am reminded of a conversation I had with a friend not too long ago. At the time, Hugo Chavez, the President of Venezuela, was getting a lot of negative press. When my wife, kids and I arrived for dinner one evening at our friend's home, she was fuming over a story she had just watched on CNN about Mr. Chavez: "I can't believe that Hugo Chavez character, I thoroughly despise that man!" Not having followed the story I was surprised at the intensity of her emotion. I asked her, "Do you know him personally? Has he ever done anything intentionally to cause you harm or upset?" To this she replied, "Of course not, but all you have to do is watch the news and you would know!" So I responded, "Let me see if I've got this right. You have some very intense animosity and dislike towards someone whom you've never met and has done absolutely nothing to you. This is all based on some news stories you've heard, and you have no idea if they are true or not? Doesn't that scare you? Look at the intensity of your emotions and the amount of judgment you have towards this man. Don't you realize that this is all based on hearsay?" After a brief pause she replied, "Well, if you watched the news more often and were better informed on what is going on in the world, you would understand why I feel the way I do!" "Exactly!" I exclaimed. "Now you know why I don't watch the news. If this is the price you pay to be informed, what is the benefit? All I can see is that you are emotionally upset over something you have no control over, and you have no idea as to whether or not it is even true. What's the point? How is this serving you in any positive way?" To this my friend said, "Can we just drop the subject and enjoy our dinner?" To this I said, "Sure, do you have any Chardonnay open?"

One of the dilemmas we face is finding a balance between keeping aware of national and world events, and not getting sucked into the maelstrom of negativity and distortion. It helps to keep in mind that the stories in the mainstream news media are often biased. The disproportionate amount of attention that is paid to negative occurrences is not an accurate reflection of the typical goings on in our world. I am reminded once again of the lesson that was shared by the visitor (spirit keeper) from the west. "Not everything is as it appears, so don't be too quick to judge or jump to conclusions." No matter how it may appear, God is always in the center of everything. Remember this, bless everything, and do not take life so seriously.

Thoughts on Leadership

A good leader is someone you feel like you work with, not for.

Unlike many folks that I know, I really enjoy my job. For nearly 25 years I have been extremely blessed to have worked for NASA at Ames Research Center. During that time, I've had the pleasure and good fortune to be involved with many exciting programs such as Galileo, Cassini, Space Station, Mars Exploration Rovers, Stardust, and Deep Impact. It has been an honor to work with many wonderful, brilliant people. Also during that time I've observed a number of approaches to supervisory positions and have come to the conclusion that there are managers and there are leaders. By my definition, managers apply more of a mechanistic approach to directing and supervising their employees. They assign and utilize employees like resources to complete tasks and solve problems. An effective manager also possesses sound organizational skills and a relevant technical background. Leaders, on the other hand, take things a step further by incorporating a human element in their approach. Building upon the aforementioned managerial skills, a leader is also adept at establishing rapport, motivating and developing employees, and has good communication skills.

I have worked for both managers and leaders and have found it considerably easier to sustain high levels of motivation and productivity working for a leader. For 16 years I was extremely fortunate to have such a leader as my supervisor. I learned much from his example, which helped to shape my own approach to the roll of supervisor. Although this roll is still a work in progress, the leadership style that I aspire to emulate is most eloquently described by Lao Tzu in the Tao Te Ching.

Leading by Example (The Master doesn't talk, he acts): We often look around us wishing we could change this person or that person, but the reality is we can only change ourselves. Folks change if and only if they want to change. The only thing any of us can really do is to lead by example, and even then there is no guarantee that change will occur. Once again it's like leading the proverbial horse to water. However, if you move through the world in a way that is positive, respectful and empowering, it

When the master governs,
the people are hardly
aware he exists.
Next best is a leader
who is loved.
Next, one who is feared.
The worst is
one who is despised.

If you don't trust the people,
you make them untrustworthy.

The Master doesn't talk, he acts.
When his work is done,
the people say. "Amazing:
we did it, all by ourselves!"

tends to rub off on those around you, simply because folks feel good being in your presence. They don't necessarily know why, but they start to emulate facets of your way of being. I think Gandhi said it best "be the change you wish to see." Folks are much more likely to do as you do, than they are to do as you say.

Empowering those you lead (Amazing: we did it, all by ourselves!): In any group or team situation it is common for the group to be presented with opportunities to head down the path of complaining and bemoaning. At times like these, I try to validate the feelings of my team members, yet gently remind them that blaming and complaining serve no productive purpose. I then try to redirect the focus towards finding solutions rather than complaining about problems or pointing fingers. Sometimes I'm successful in doing this, sometime I'm not. Also, I strive to treat my team members with respect and I value their input. Anyone and everyone can come up with a good idea. I encourage them to utilize their talents and tell them, "If you see something that needs fixing, fix it! If you see something that can be improved and you have an idea on how to improve it, then let's talk about it. If it looks viable, then be ready to take on that task as your special project." I have found that when folks become actively involved with, and take ownership of, seeking solutions to what they perceive to be problems they spend far less time complaining. If folks feel empowered and valued, they tend to be more productive and happy.

In addition, when situations or requirements arise that appear to be rather nonsensical or none too wise, I remind my team members that usually one of two things is going on. Either the situation or requirement is silly and nobody has invested the effort to find a better alternative, or we are simply not aware of all the underlying details. I have learned from experience not to be too quick to judge something because odds are I only have a superficial understanding of the situation. Appearances can be misleading. In short, I like to empower my team members and encourage them to be drivers in this ride we call life instead of passengers.

Prior to pursuing a recent job opportunity within my division, I led a team that was made up of highly skilled, dedicated, hard working, innovative, productive and fun individuals. As the team leader I tried to apply the principles and approaches outlined above. As a result, our team was efficient, productive and had excellent team chemistry where the performance of the team as a whole far outweighed the sum of its individual parts. Leadership was certainly an important part of the equation, yet there were other important parts as well. These included the mix of personality types, and years of working together which fostered good communication and shared experiences to draw from to solve problems. I certainly made mistakes along the way, and grew from these, and I found that like many aspects of life the roll of leader is a journey not a destination.

I have learned that a good leader takes time to get to know all of the members of his or her team, and becomes familiar with their strengths and shortcomings. By doing so, he or she can then assign these individuals to positions that best utilize their strengths while at the same time providing them a means to develop their weaknesses. A good leader also tries to provide his or her team members with all the resources they need to thrive at their positions. A leader who does this and is honest and straightforward, earns the trust and respect of his or her team members. Team members that trust and respect their leadership are more dedicated and hard working than those who do not. Imagine what the world would be like if political leadership typically aspired to emulate the suggestions by Lao Tzu?

Clutter
and
Chaos

*Often there are many means
to the same end.
In these situations, choose the path of
least resistance and save your energy for
activities that make your heart sing.*

Complaining doesn't solve problems nor does it serve any constructive purpose. When confronted with a situation that I don't like, I give myself two choices: either change the situation or change my attitude. This has been my mantra throughout most of my adult life and it has served me quite well. One situation I find challenging is coping with a cluttered and disorganized environment. I prefer to live in an environment that is orderly, clean, comfortable, inviting and devoid of clutter. Although I am not a clean freak, I am a well-organized minimalist. However, I've had occasions to live with people who are the antithesis of this. Most of the clutter-prone folks I know dislike this element of their way of being, but are uncertain how to change it. One popular misconception about such folks is that they are lazy. On the contrary, most of the clutter-prone folks I know are extremely hard working and busy individuals. However, it is their lack of consistency and self-discipline that results in choices which makes life much more difficult than it need be. They end up creating more work for themselves and the tasks of getting and staying organized become insurmountable.

In contrast, I have observed that non-clutter prone folks have several simple habits. I follow these habits and have found them to be very effective at keeping clutter to a minimum, if not eliminating it altogether. These habits do require self-discipline and consistency. Ask anyone who is non-clutter-prone and they will tell you, the way to eliminate clutter and chaos is not by working harder, but by working smarter.

Habits of "Non-Clutter-Prone" People

Put things away right away; don't set things down. By doing just this one thing, you can avoid clutter from the get go. It sounds simple enough, and it is but it requires giving up the habit of being a "dropper." What is a "dropper?" A dropper is an individual that as soon as they walk through the door they set down whatever they are carrying on the nearest open counter top, table top or even the floor. They figure they'll put it away later. Unfortunately, later doesn't usually come until nearly every square inch of horizontal surface is piled deep in stuff, or guests are soon to arrive. Then the stuff typically gets whisked away into a bag or box to, once again, be dealt with at some later time. Often the dropper has bags or boxes that are years old waiting for a magical day to arrive when they will have ample time to deal with them. For the "dropper" every flat surface is a place for stuff to be set upon. The world is their aircraft carrier and they land often. This more than anything is the genesis of clutter, so it is a habit that must be broken.

Put things in the same place. Once you find a home for an item be sure to put it there whenever it is not in use. We've all seen frenzied searches for misplaced car keys, cell phones, shoes, toothbrushes, and clothing items. These panicked fits of hysteria could easily be avoided if folks simply put their items away in the same place as soon as they finish using them. This sounds simple, and it is, but like any habit it requires developing consistency. This approach eliminates all the time wasted on wild goose chases looking for lost items. Also, if you have small children in your household, be sure to put important items in places they

can't get to. Kids are amazingly curious and what's even more amazing is their ability to find and hide things.

Open one package at a time, and finish it before opening another. This is yet another simple thing to do, yet, it makes a big difference in the amount of clutter that accumulates. For example, if you are thirsty and get a bottle of drinking water from your pantry, finish it before getting another one. If you need to set it down before you finish it, either put it in a place you will remember, or mark it in some manner, peel or draw on the label, so you can identify it. I've lived in situations where on any given day you are likely to find something like ten bottles of water in various stages of fullness (notice I didn't say emptiness) scattered about the place. Often it is unclear whose bottle is whose or how long each bottle has been open. As a result, a lot of water gets poured down the drain. This is wasteful, creates clutter, and if there are small children in the household they will invariably get ahold of the bottles and spill them onto the floors, furniture, or heat registers. This, of course, creates more interesting and unnecessary messes to be cleaned up. A few water bottles by themselves are no big deal, but when you add to the picture cereal boxes, containers of diaper wipes, juice boxes, boxes of crackers and so on, you end up with quite a bit of clutter in short order. Clutter is about volume and when you have many redundant items, you significantly increase the potential for clutter.

Think containment. My wife and I have three beautiful children under the age of eight. If left to their own devices they will take their snacks and meal items to every corner of our home, scattering crumbs, spills and such all along their merry way. Messes abound, yet they don't have to. Let's face it: children are going to make messes, especially when they eat. It's part of learning and growing. Yet, if snacks and meals are kept at a table or breakfast counter, it contains the fallout and makes cleaning up much less involved and arduous. It's a simple thing but it makes a noticeable difference in the amount of time and effort spent cleaning up after munchkins. Some of these munchkins grow up and continue to behave in the same manner, so this same rule applies to adults as well.

Don't be a pack rat! Every time my family has moved we've always ended up with a collection of boxes that we never seem to have time to unpack, organize and put away. This is not at all uncommon and there's a good reason why this happens to folks. Most of this boxed up stuff is unnecessary! Think about it: when you move you typically unpack and put away the stuff you need for daily use. The rest of the stuff, that is the stuff that stays in boxes for years, realistically could be gotten rid of with no appreciable affect on quality of life. So, why not do this? Why is it so difficult for folks to part with stuff they never use? Obviously, if they really need this stuff, it would be unpacked and used with some degree of regularity. For example, I know some folks who have an old rocking chair that was supposedly made by a distant relative during the Civil War. It needs wood work and reupholstering to be useable. However, its style doesn't go with their home decor. So what's the point of hanging on to this old rocking chair? It only takes up space and continues to deteriorate in their garage. Why not sell it or donate it, and other similar things, so that they can actually park a car in their garage? A good rule of thumb is if you haven't used something in more than a year or two, you probably don't need it. Some folks are fearful that as soon as they get rid of something they will find that they need it. The counter argument to this is, until you get rid of things, odds are you probably don't remember you have these things and if you do you probably can't remember where they are anyway. One of the benefits about being a minimalist is that the fewer things you have, the fewer things there are to create clutter.

Clean as you go and be mindful of the consequences of your choices. A classic example of this is how you operate in a kitchen. I once had two roommates, both of whom were very good cooks. Roommate number 1 cooked with reckless

abandon and when dinner was served it was a culinary treat indeed. However, when the meal was over, clean-up was a nightmare. Our kitchen typically looked like a bomb had gone off. Nearly every utensil, pot and pan had been used and there were splashes and spills on the counter tops, cabinets, floors and sometimes even the ceiling (I kid you not). In contrast, roommate number 2 could prepare the same dish, taking slightly more time, but was mindful not to spill and would clean as she went. When dinner was served it was equally as satisfying. However, cleaning up after this roommate was a breeze. Initially, we all took turns cooking and our rule was if you cooked you didn't have to do the dishes. After a few months, roommate number 2 and I were getting quite tired of roommate number 1 turning our kitchen into a FEMA disaster site. After much discussion we changed the rule to, whoever cooks also cleans. This was a win-win situation. Roommate number 1 could continue to cook in whatever manner he desired and his actions no longer affected roommate number 2 or me. Often there are many means to the same end. Choose the path of least resistance. Save your energy for activities that make your heart sing.

Finish what you start. During high school I took woodshop, metalshop and autoshop and my instructors always stressed, "A project isn't complete until all the tools are put away and the work site is cleaned up." So when you start a project, follow it through to its completion including cleaning up. If you are about to begin a new project, be realistic with your estimate as to how long it is going to take. If you don't have time to complete the project in a reasonable amount of time, consider saving it for another day. If you get too many projects going at the same time, you tend to work inefficiently, you lose momentum, the projects stall and often they remain incomplete indefinitely. If you have several projects in the works, finish at least some them before you start new ones. Incomplete projects that sit around for a prolonged period of time, and not cleaning up promptly, are additional sources of clutter.

Like all habits, these take time and repetition before they become ingrained in our subconscious. So take your time and don't be too hard on yourself when you find that you are reverting back to old ways. Simply dust yourself off and begin again. Developing these habits will go a long way in transforming a clutter-prone person into a non-clutter-prone person.

When I lived with clutter-prone roommates, I tried to lead by example. I took the Gandhi approach and tried to be the change I wanted to see by modeling the behavior I wanted to take root. This typically resulted in little or no change on my roommates' part, and a lot of frustration on my part. I often found myself biting my tongue and muttering under my breath things like "If you would simply rinse out your cereal bowl after you finish eating, it wouldn't take a bloody jack-hammer to get it clean!" In hindsight I realize the error of my ways. First of all, I didn't discuss with these roommates how their clutter-prone habits were affecting me in a negative manner. Second, I lost sight of the fact that folks change if and only if they want to change. Third, I didn't take the time to respectfully share alternative ways for them to consider. Most importantly, however, I was approaching the situation from an attitude of judgment, not love. This is always much more likely to cause folks to react defensively, rather than being open to suggestions.

Feng Shui and Quantum Mechanics and Ch'i

Many cultures throughout the world have come to believe in a vital life force or energy that flows within all beings and the environment. In China this is called ch'i, in India it's prana, in the west it's spirit, to the Native American it's breath, and so on. The mystical realization that we are all luminous energetic beings living in an infinite realm of energy has been espoused for millennia. The advent of quantum physics now provides a scientific underpinning that agrees with this notion. Specifically, it is recognized that what we perceive as solid matter is not really solid at all. Atoms are not hard little spheres with smaller spheres (electrons) orbiting around them. The fact is, atoms are 99% empty space, and as you go smaller in scale you find that at a fundamental level everything is made up of energy, and is part of one vast energy field. So, whether you approach it from a scientific or spiritual perspective, both agree that although each of us is an individualized expression within our environment, we are not separate from it or each other. Rather, we are an interconnected whole, we are one.

For thousands of years many folks have been acutely aware that their environment can affect their state of being. For example, a space that is warm, inviting, clean, and orderly tends to be very comfortable and uplifting. It feels good to be in this kind of space and it promotes feelings of contentment and joy. Conversely, a space that is cold, dirty, chaotic or smelly tends to be uncomfortable and depressing. Periods of time spent in this type of space can be draining, irritating and unpleasant. This awareness of environment affecting state of being has given rise to the development of practices such as Feng Shui. The primary goal of this ancient Chinese discipline is to arrange one's living space so that it is in harmony with the natural environment. This allows for an optimal flow of energy (ch'i) through the space, which in turn promotes good health, wealth and well being. Over the centuries, many Feng Shui techniques have been established that provide guidance in the layout and arrangement of a home, and the placement of furniture and such within a home. The goal is to foster optimal ch'i, or energy flow within the home. Keep in mind that many of these traditions predate electricity, plumbing, central heating, insulation and other modern building practices. Hence, some of the details of the older traditions may be less applicable today than they used to be. As always when dealing with ancient matters, it is important to recognize the intention that underlies the details and to not get fixated on the details themselves. The main point is that your living space does have an affect on your state of being. In various Feng Shui books I've noticed that even though there are differences in the details, they all speak to the ill effects of clutter. In other words, the beneficial effects of arranging your home for optimal ch'i can be severely negated by the presence of persistent clutter.

It's a Two-way Street

In addition to the environment having an affect on people, people can have an energetic affect on their environment. For example, most folks have probably experienced entering a room just after two people have had a very intense disagreement. Without any words being spoken or facial expressions being observed, you can sense the tension in the air. It's palpable. Similarly, there are some folks that have such a powerfully positive vibe about them that whenever they enter a room folks feel uplifted just by their presence. I imagine this must have been the experience to be in the presence of Buddha and Jesus. Conversely, there are folks who can suck the life out of a room when they enter it, such as intimidators and "poor me" (perpetual victim) types. Thus, energy flow is omni directional and flows through and between all things. How is your environment affecting you, and how are you effecting your environment?

What does it all mean?

There is compelling evidence that it is in your own best interest to be comfortable in your environment. In particular, your home should be a positive enjoyable space to be in. You spend a great deal of time there and how you feel while you are there affects the atmosphere of your thoughts. As mentioned previously, the atmosphere of your thoughts shapes the reality you experience. Thus, it shouldn't come as a surprise to discover that the place you call home has a profound effect on your well being. By transforming clutter and chaos into orderliness and harmony you will undoubtedly find yourself happier and healthier as a result. Of course your ability to do this is constrained by the nature and number of people you live with. If you find yourself in a living situation where maintaining order and harmony seem beyond your control, where you often feel as though you are rearranging the furniture on the deck of the Titanic, do not despair for all is not lost. Your steadfast intention, lovingly exemplified may inspire those around you. Yet, if it does not there still can be a way out of this predicament.

If you look closely at the lives of the great mystics through the ages, it becomes clear that they achieved a level of self mastery where they were able to move through life with grace and dignity in a state of joy, vitality and inner peace that was seemingly immune to external circumstances. This same transcendent ability, through an expanded level of consciousness, is available and attainable to each of us. I'm not saying this is easy, yet it is a possibility, and whenever possibility exists so too does hope. Remember it was Siddhartha Guatama the man who became the Buddha, just as Yeshua the man became Jesus the

Christ. One thing that all mystics have in common is that they were ordinary people who achieved an extraordinary state of consciousness. As mystics in training, we too can follow in their footsteps. We can evolve our beliefs and opinions and change our reactions to our circumstances. We can go beyond "seek first the kingdom" and become permanent residents there.

This is one of my current intentions. I am striving to attain and sustain that state wherein my environment, wherever I may happen to be, no longer adversely affects me. To this end I am a work in progress. What I have found to be effective so far is to take every day and every moment one step at a time, and not get too hung up on how I am actually spending my time. I try to be as helpful as I can, realizing this is my nature. I also try to set aside some time for myself. When I find that I am engaged in repetitive activities that seem to be futile, I remind myself of the Buddhist wisdom of seeking to find the point of pointlessness.

There are times where I find that I am haunted by the words and wisdom of my good friend, Rev. Jane Beach, "View every situation as though you chose it." Admittedly sometimes my reaction is "Why the heck would I choose this? Only a complete moron would choose this! I didn't choose this!!!" On such occasions, I pause, breathe, and remind myself "You live in the kingdom now. Here is another opportunity to remember that." So, I look around at the situation and I say, "This is an occasion to prove to myself that I can do this. I too can be like Buddha and Jesus! I can be blissful in any circumstance be it walking on the beach, sitting in my medicine wheel, driving in rush hour traffic or wading through a cesspool of sh… clutter. The choice is mine and I am the master of my choices." In so doing, I'm finding that the more often I am successful the easier it is becoming.

The Journey Continues

*If you look deeply enough at all
that surrounds you, you will find
that it's all the same gift but with
different wrapping paper*

As mentioned at the outset, a mystic is a person that develops a genuine mastery of life, and recognizes that both the human and transcendent experiences are precious, and that each of us has been given the capacity and a predisposition to experience both fully. Those of us who choose to actively engage in cultivating such a life are indeed mystics in training. We seek to satisfy our innate hunger to wake up, to discern who we are and why we are here, and to partake in the continuing quest for authentic self-discovery and expression. As we immerse ourselves in this awakening process, we find that there is so much more to life than what we perceive with our five outward focused senses. As we stretch our consciousness, and peer beneath the veil of religious dogma to examine underlying spiritual principals and universal truths, we begin to experience a heightened recurrence of synchronicity and a conspicuous sense of unity. We begin to quench our thirst for illumination as we imbibe the limitless waters of enlightenment.

A Curious Dream

I once had a dream where all the members of humanity were treading water in a vast sea that stretched beyond the limits of sight in every direction. In general, folks were unaware that they were treading water and were completely content and convinced that the surface of this vast sea fully defined the realities of existence. Yet, every so often, an individual would awaken to the awareness that there was something beneath the surface. Bravely, they would dive into the mysterious depths and begin to explore this new realm, the realm of enlightenment. From time to time they would resurface and share their new found insights with those treading water. Most of the surface dwellers would smile and dismiss the explorer's tales as flights of fancy. Yet some would feel inspired and soon would follow suit. Gradually, the number of enlightened explorers grew until a critical mass was achieved. At that point, there was a shift in the collective consciousness and all of humanity became aware of the enlightened realm. So dawned a new day in human consciousness, and so began a new paradigm, the next step in human evolution.

Final Comments

In 1994, fueled by inspiration, I began my quest for authentic self discovery and expression, and an enlightened way of being. This path of the mystic in training is truly the birthright of anyone who chooses to engage in it. One of the tangible benefits I have received, and continue to receive, is a steadily increasing mastery of my life. There now exists a very real undercurrent of love, joy and inner peace that is proving to be independent of external circumstances. It is definitely palpable and not as easily obscured by the vicissitudes of life. Although I feel like I've just scratched the surface, my beliefs, perceptions, and philosophies have evolved dramatically, and consciously. Some of the resulting "ah ha" moments that have occurred so far have served as the basis for the discussions in this book. These rest stops along the journey are admittedly quite varied, yet such is the nature of the grand tapestry of life and all of its wondrous diversity.

For anyone who chooses to walk the path of the mystic in training, it is a truly a way of life and not something that is reserved for Sundays or when you are sitting on a meditation cushion. Whether your journey is by way of the good red road, new thought ancient wisdom teachings, or any other faith tradition that truly sings to your head and heart, what you ultimately discover is that when you peel back the layers of surface appearances everything in life is divine at its core. From the mundane to the sublime all beings, things, situations and circumstances are imbued with the essence of the Great Spirit, for God is truly omnipresent.

My sincere hope is that you enjoyed reading this book as much as I enjoyed writing it and that it catalyzed some of your own musings, ponderings and insights. I must admit, looking back at the way the chapters unfolded, I often felt like an observer in that they were happening through me rather than by me. In other words, it often seemed that I was not the doer, just the vehicle for the chapters to surface. The gentle voice was right. I started writing and the words flowed. Once again I can sense that voice whispering my ear and this time it is saying, "it is done, for now." This leads me to believe that there are more books to be written for this walk is truly infinite in its possibilities and opportunities. For now, though, this first experience has reached a nice stopping point. If I've learned anything during my travels, it is to trust that inner voice.

Epilogue:

Moments
of
Inspiration

*Dark chocolate and
ruby port are a fantastic
combination that often
leads to epiphany
and inspiration*

Over the last several years, I've experienced flashes of insight in the form of catch phrases or divinely inspired one liner's. So, I took to the habit of writing them down for nothing other than recording them for my own amusement and contemplation. Little did I realize that many of these truisms would serve as befitting precursors for the chapters of this book? Spirit certainly works in interesting ways! What follows here is a list of twenty-six of some of the most memorable moments of inspiration to date. Enjoy!

1   In Life there are no final destinations, only points along an endless journey.

2   The world is a big place, yet truth is truth no matter where you are.

3   All paths can lead to God.

4   Rituals and ceremonies can be useful tools for worship, but they themselves should never be worshiped.

5   God has never stopped talking, but many folks have forgotten how to listen.

6   Contrary to popular belief, it takes a tremendous amount of faith to be an Atheist.

7   Spirituality is God's essence, Religion is man's interpretation.

8   It's not a question of choosing between God and Science, rather, it's about recognizing that God is Science.

9   Jesus and Darwin are the best of friends.

10   Life is an unending series of choices and results.

11   Often we focus too much on symptoms and not enough on root causes.

12   If it doesn't make your heart sing, why do it?

13 A good leader is someone you feel like you work with, not for.

14 Often there are many means to the same end. In these situations, choose the path of least resistance and save your energy for activities that make your heart sing.

15 Dark chocolate and ruby port are a fantastic combination that often leads to epiphany and inspiration.

16 If you look deeply enough at all that surrounds you, you will find that it's all the same gift but with different wrapping paper.

17 At any given moment, more than likely, some folks think you're an angel, and others think you're an a-hole. Hopefully there's more of the angel contingent.

18 You don't have to be ignorant to be blissful, but it often makes it easier.

19 Sometimes it can be hard to find, but there is always a silver lining.

20 The first step toward world peace is to be a peaceful individual.

21 Money neither ensures nor precludes happiness. It merely enables a wider array of potential experiences.

22 Good is the essence of our spirit, evil is a product of our ego.

23 God doesn't judge or punish, people do.

24 If people were not intended to enjoy sex, it wouldn't be so enjoyable!

25 Opportunity is forever knocking.

26 Luminosity is love made visible.

Acknowledgements

First and foremost, I would like to acknowledge and express my gratitude to the Great Spirit for the gifts of life, love, inspiration and creativity. I would also like to thank my beautiful wife and each of my children, my parents and extended family, and my many dear friends for all of their love, support and encouragement. Love is boundless in its variety of forms and expressions, and is most obviously experienced through relationships. So to all of those folks whom I've had the honor of crossing paths with during my life's journey, I thank you for allowing me the opportunity to experience so many expressions of love. During my life I have found many sources of inspiration. There are individuals that I know personally and there are those whom I've never met, but whose works inspire me greatly. To all of the teachers, mentors, authors, poets, musicians, artists, and angels that have touched my life, I sincerely thank you for making this human experience truly awesome.

About the author

CJ Cornelison was born in California. His father vanished from his life when he was four years old. He spent his summers in Rhode Island from age 2 to 15 with his grandparents whose unconditional love, acceptance and understanding had a profound influence on him. He was supported to be in Boy Scouts and in his teens became an Eagle Scout, and learned to love the outdoors throughout his childhood in California and his summers in Rhode Island. The steadfast love and support of his mother and stepfather have anchored him throughout his life, yet CJ now realizes that from an early age he subconsciously sought information about his Native American heritage as a way of connecting with his father and his own roots. The ceremonies and traditions he learned guided him to spiritual concepts that resonated with him at a deep level and that lead him onto other paths of self discovery.

He went to U.C. Davis where he received B.S. degree, and then, Stanford University a M.S. degree, both in mechanical engineering. Recently he became a licensed Religious Science Practitioner (RScP).

He is married to Heidi (his best friend), and has four great children, Kevin, Joey, Charlie and Natalie.

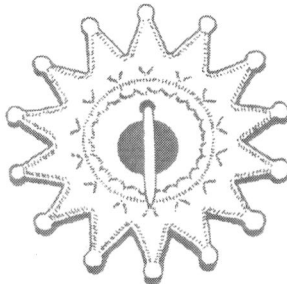